HOME-STYLE
COOKING

SIMPLE, EASY AND DELICIOUS

BY SHARON WONG

Pictured on Front Cover; also pictured on page 71:
(top to bottom) Lemon Chicken Breast, page 68; Daikon and Vermicelli Soup, page 15; Green Pepper and Soy Sauce Beef, page 79; Zucchini Onion with Pork, page 91; Cauliflower with Tomato Sauce, page 39; Ginger Pork with Tofu, page 59; Oriental Pork Noodles, page 48.

Chinese Home-Style Cooking
by
Sharon Wong

First Printing — August 1996

Canadian Cataloguing in Publication Data

Wong, Sharon, 1952-
    Chinese home-style cooking

      Includes index.
      ISBN 1-895292-80-8

1. Cookery, Chinese. I. Title.

TX724.5.C5W66 1996   641.5951   C96-920101-X

Photography by:
Qinglai Zhang
Regina, Saskatchewan

Cover and page design by:
Brian Danchuk
Brian Danchuk Design
Regina, Saskatchewan

Designed, Printed and Produced in Canada by:
Centax, Books, A Division of PrintWest Communications
Publishing Director – Margo Embury
1150 Eighth Avenue, Regina, Saskatchewan
Canada S4R 1C9
(306)525-2304 Fax (306)757-2439

Table of Contents

Recipes have been tested in U.S standard measurements. The rounded metric equivalents are given for those cooks who are more comfortable with metric.

Foreword

Sharon Wong

"Chinese food is delicious to eat but hard to cook." Many of my Canadian friends have made this comment. However, this is not true. Chinese meals, especially Chinese family meals, are delicious to eat and easy to cook. Nowadays, most people would rather not spend too much time cooking; they have so many responsibilities, working outside the home, as well as child care and housework. Even for entertaining at home, few people wish to spend long hours cooking. They dream of preparing the most delicious meal in the least amount of time.

Ever since I was a child growing up in China, I cooked for my family. My parents were preoccupied with their jobs and could not return home in time to cook. Thus, I became the "cook" in the family. Like any other child I preferred to play with my friends rather than spend time in the kitchen, so I learned to prepare appropriate meals in the least amount of time. My father enjoyed cooking and in his spare time he was a wonderful cook. On holidays and special occasions, he prepared delicious meals for the entire family. I was appointed his assistant and I learned a lot from him. At that time I tried to read many cookbooks, picking up skills and recipes as we went along. The end result was delicious and beautifully prepared meals.

My life experience has been rich indeed. For many years I lived in the Chinese countryside where supplies were very simple: only corn, yellow beans, salt and some cooking oil. I learned to cook using very little. I then moved to a factory where I cooked for more than a thousand people every day. After I arrived in Canada I was employed as a cook in a popular Chinese restaurant.

In spite of my varied cooking experience, I am not a professional chef. I have a university degree in engineering, and once lectured in computer science. Now that I am married and have a family, cooking plays a more important part in my life. Evening and weekend meals are a meaningful time for our family. Cooking is a way of expressing my love to my husband and my daughter. I know many Canadian families experience or wish to experience these feelings.

When friends ask me how to cook, I simply share with them my cooking skills. Often they are surprised at how easy and time-saving it is to cook a delicious Chinese meal. "It is so simple, I could make it too!" they say. I am overwhelmed when my Canadian friends tell me that they are cooking a delicious Chinese meal that they learned from me.

I would like to share with you my *Chinese Home-Style Cooking*, especially with those of you who love Chinese food but have never cooked it before. When you follow my simple instructions, step by step, you will have a delicious Chinese meal in 15-20 minutes.

For these recipes, I have chosen meat, vegetables and seasonings that are suitable for Western tastes. All the ingredients, meat and vegetables, are available at your local grocery store. The utensils are the ones you use in your daily cooking. You do not need a Chinese wok. I have also included colorful photographs for all the dishes you will be preparing.

I am sure if you add one or two Chinese dishes to your daily menu, your family and friends will be delighted. I hope that my recipes will bring happiness and harmony to you and your family. It is an honor to share them with you.

Sharon Wong

Acknowledgements

This very special Chinese cookbook combines the wisdom of experts and of many friends. I wish to sincerely and publicly thank them for playing an important role in my book.

I thank my dear husband, my daughter, my sister, Lili, and brother, Yan. Their support and encouragement made me diligent and confident.

Special thanks to my best friends:
Evangeline and Bingsu Shen
Merv and Carol Hepting
Laurene Bitz
Mike and Kelli Poehlmann
Alvin and Shelby Gryba
Bob and Wanda Ursulescu
Pastor Les Skonnord and Betty Skonnord (Thunder Bay);

They gave me valuable suggestions in regard to writing the book, recipe testing, photography, book publishing and even in computer typing.

And hearty thanks to:
Pastor Ron Phillips and Argyle Road Baptist Church (Regina);
Connaught Library and Conversation Group (Regina);
Holy Trinity Anglican Church;
For their concern, support and blessing.

I would like to particularly thank my book's editor, Margo Embury, and publishing assistant Iona Glabus.

The Versatility of Chinese Home-Style Cooking

Since my recipes are designed especially for families, they are flexible. Cooking at home is not like cooking in a restaurant. Most of the time you may not prepare a recipe exactly as it is written in a cookbook. You may adapt it to suit the ingredients you have on hand and your family's tastes.

When you choose a recipe to cook at home, sometimes you discover that you lack some ingredients such as a flavoring or specific vegetable. Don't worry; in my recipes you can use another ingredient instead of the one specified. For example, if you want to cook a pork meatball soup, but you do not have cucumber, it is not a problem. You can substitute diced tomato and the flavor will be still very good.

Some seasonings, such as ginger and green onion, you can adjust according to your and your family's tastes. In China, people usually use more ginger in cooking. It has the special function of driving cold out from your body, so it is a natural and healthy food.

I have found that many Canadian friends like onion very much. According to modern scientific research, onion may help treat diseases of the heart and blood vessels. So add a little more onion to your meals for good flavor and good health.

One thing you should pay attention to is the amount of salt in your meal. You can adjust amounts to suit your taste.

In brief, in my Chinese family cookbook you can change amounts of ingredients according to your needs and taste and still make the meal delicious and tasty. This is the difference between Chinese family cooking and Chinese restaurant dishes. I believe that if you follow the family recipes, making small changes as needed or desired, you will create flavorful, enjoyable dishes.

Cooking Hints

Broccoli

Broccoli, with its bright color and many nutrients, is an important ingredient in many meals. Here is a way to lightly cook it to be used either hot or cold. Boil enough water to cover the broccoli in a saucepan. Add 1 tbsp. (15 mL) salt and 1 tbsp. (15 mL) vegetable oil to the boiling water. Add the broccoli and boil for 2 minutes. The broccoli's color becomes emerald green and it looks very fresh.

Ginger Root

Ginger root is one of the most popular seasonings in Chinese cooking. Storing it is very simple. When you buy some fresh ginger, wrap it in a plastic bag such as a sandwich bag, seal the bag and put it into the refrigerator. Close the bag tightly each time you use the ginger. Keep it cool to avoid drying and mildew. For longer storage, ginger freezes well in an airtight container. Grate or shave while still frozen. However, there is some flavor loss when ginger is frozen, so increase the amount to your taste.

Onions, Slicing

The volatile elements of cut onion stimulate the eyes and cause tears. To avoid this, before you cut the onion, put the knife in cold water for a second. If you didn't take care and your eyes are tearing, remember not to use your hand to rub your eyes. Stand in a ventilated cool place for a while or look at the cool water for a moment. Chilling the onion before slicing and also putting a piece of bread near the chopping board (to absorb odors) are recommended by some cooks as eye-saving measures.

Rice, Burnt

One familiar kitchen problem is burnt rice. Both the smell and the flavor of burnt rice can be dealt with very simply. **Do not stir!** First, set a bowl of cold water on top of the burnt rice; cover the pot and let it sit for 5–10 minutes. Remove the cover and the burnt smell will be gone. Second, to rescue the flavor of burnt rice, put some chopped white or green onion on top of the rice and cover again. Before serving, remove the onion and the rice is ready to eat.

Rice, Partially Cooked

Sometimes when you are cooking rice, you may put in less water than you are supposed to, or the steam may push off the lid and the water may boil over, resulting in too little water. If this happens, DO NOT add cold water to the pot. Add HOT water. Prior to adding water, poke some holes in the rice with a fork, just so the water will seep through. Cover, then bring the water to a boil again over low heat and continue cooking until the rice is done. If there happens to be too much water in the pot, just spoon it out.

Tofu

Tofu, made from soybeans, is a natural and healthy food. It contains high amounts of plant albumen and many vitamins and amino acids. High in protein, it has no cholesterol. Tofu absorbs the flavors of the foods it is cooked with so it is very versatile. It comes in silken, medium and firm textures; all should be stored covered with water which is changed every day. Tofu can be frozen for up to 3 months, with a resulting chewier texture. Tofu can be diced, sliced or mashed and used in stir-fries, soups, salads, casseroles and sauces.

In Chinese family meals, tofu is enjoyed by young and old, but some people do not like the odor of it cooking. To dispel odor and make the tofu fresh and flavorful, just put it in boiling water for 2–3 minutes before cooking with it.

Stir-Frying

Stir-frying in a little hot oil is a traditional and important skill in Chinese cooking. The dishes are delicious and tender-crisp. Chopped vegetables and meats are quickly cooked by constant stirring over very high heat. This method drains air from inside the vegetables, making them translucent and the colors very bright. Vegetables such as cucumbers, celery and cabbage are green because of chlorophyll, which is an unstable pigment. If it is heated for a long time the chlorophyll molecule loses magnesium and the vegetables change to a tawny color.

The greatest loss, however, would be of the vitamins in vegetables. A short cooking time can preserve many of them, up to 60–70% of the vitamin C and also some of the riboflavin and carotene.

Stir-Frying Tips

Many people are nervous when they start to learn how to cook Chinese food. Especially when the pot is heated, the oil is sizzling and they suddenly forget what they need to do. But there is no time to read the recipe over again, so everything gets confusing. Sometimes when the cooking is finished, they find vegetables or spices that have been left out. Here are some helpful tips.

1. You've got to know the recipe very well, so you should read it over a couple of times.

2. Prepare the things you need before you cook. Put everything in separate containers, then arrange the containers in order, first, second, third . . . in 1 line. If the recipe tells you to add the spices without telling you which to put in first, then put them all together before cooking. For example: If a dish has meat and vegetables:

oil in frying pan	minced onion or ginger	meat	veget-ables	sauce	serving dish

3. It is important to follow the recipe step by step, putting in ingredients one after the other.

If you follow the tips I have given you, I promise that you will be able to make a delicious meal without frustration.

Oil Fire – Safety Note

With hot oil in a frying pan or wok, there is always the possibility of an oil fire. If a fire should occur, DO NOT TRY TO DROWN IT WITH WATER. Put a cover over the pan to cut off the oxygen supply to the fire OR smother the fire by adding chopped vegetables to the pan.

The Basics

Boiled Rice

| 2 cups | long-grain rice | 500 mL |
| 3 cups | water | 750 mL |

1. Wash rice until water is clear in saucepan. Drain. Add the 3 cups (750 mL) of water, or use your finger to measure depth of water. If the water is 1 knuckle of your index finger from rice to water surface, you have enough water.
2. Bring the water to boil over high heat. When water boils, turn the heat to low and leave pot uncovered for about 2 minutes.
3. Cover and cook for 20 minutes.

Serves 5 or makes approximately 5 cups (1 L) of rice.

Rice

Basic to southern Chinese cooking, plain boiled or steamed rice is an important part of every meal. Vegetables, fish and meat accompany the rice, adding flavor, nutrition and variety, but the rice is the foundation of the diet. Long-grain white rice is the most popular and is available in many varieties, as is short-grain rice. The more glutinous (sticky) varieties are mainly used for cakes and puddings. In northern China, rice is also eaten, but noodles, millet and sweet potatoes are a more important part of the daily diet.

Chicken Broth

This subtly flavored nutritious broth is a favorite in every Chinese family.

6 cups	water	1.5 L
1	whole chicken	1
2 tsp.	chopped ginger	10 mL
2 tsp.	chopped onion	10 mL
½ tsp.	salt	2 mL

1. Place water and chicken in a large saucepan over high heat. Make sure there is enough water to cover the chicken.
2. When water comes to a boil, skim froth from soup. Add ginger, onion and salt. Reduce heat to low and cover pot. Simmer for 40 minutes.
3. Remove chicken and save the chicken meat for other recipes, e.g., Peanut Butter Sesame Chicken, page 69. Strain the broth and skim off the fat. Serve the broth in small cups or bowls. Add salt to taste.

Serves 6.

Chicken Broth or Stock

Comforting and soothing to the spirit, chicken broth is used as a basic stock in many soup and stir-fry sauce recipes or as a nourishing drink. In many Chinese meals, soup is served at the end of the meal as a savory complement to the rich and complex flavors that have gone before. Breakfast may be a simple bowl of steaming chicken broth with rice or noodles added. Chicken broth is also recommended as a health drink in China; it is recommended that one drink a small cup of broth each day for healthy skin and a younger looking complexion.

Chinese Tea

This is the favorite partner with Chinese food.

| 2 tsp. | Chinese green tea | 10 mL |
| 4 cups | boiling water | 1 L (1 teapot) |

1. Put the tea into the teapot and pour the boiling water over the tea leaves. Cover and let steep for about 5 minutes.
2. If some tea leaves float, pour some water from the teapot into a cup and pour back into the teapot. Do this 2 or 3 times.

Serves 6.

Tea in Chinese Cuisine and Culture

Refreshing and relaxing, tea is a staple in Chinese homes. Consumed throughout the day and with almost every meal, tea is also a symbol of hospitality. It is offered to guests in one's home and is also an important courtesy in business transactions. Tea is traditionally sent to family members and friends as a symbol of affection, and for newlyweds it represents faithfulness and everlasting love.

Tea grew wild in China until the Chinese discovered that the tea leaves flavored boiled water and could be used for medicinal purposes. For about 2,500 years it was used as a medicinal or stimulating drink. About 1500 years ago, the pleasurable aspects of tea drinking came to be emphasized and tea cultivation spread from China to Japan and to India. The three basic types of tea are, fermented black tea, semifermented oolong tea and what most people think of as Chinese or green tea, which is unfermented. The leaves are steamed and dried. The resulting pale greenish tea provides the perfect accompaniment to the subtle or spicy flavors of Chinese food. There are many brands of green tea available, including flower-scented teas. The most popular flower teas are Jasmine, chrysanthemum, orchid and gardenia.

Shrimp with Lettuce Soup

A healthy and delicious soup.

¼ cup	peeled shrimp	50 mL
1 tsp.	cornstarch	5 mL
3	lettuce leaves*	3
1 tbsp.	finely chopped green onion	15 mL
2 cups	water	500 mL
½ tsp.	salt	2 mL
¼ tsp.	pepper	1 mL
¼ tsp.	sesame oil	1 mL

1. Mix peeled shrimp with cornstarch in a bowl.
2. Cut lettuce into 2" (5 cm) squares. Chop green onion.
3. Bring water to a boil in a saucepan over high heat. Lower heat to medium. Add shrimp and salt; cook for 3 minutes. Add lettuce. As soon as soup returns to a boil, add green onion, pepper and sesame oil. Serve immediately.

Serves 4. Pictured on page 17

* Any type of lettuce may be used in this recipe. Many supermarkets also have a varied selection of traditional Chinese greens which may be called by different names in different areas, Chinese cabbage, bok choy, baby bok choy, Chinese cole, Chinese spinach, Chinese yellow flowering vegetables, etc. Experiment with a variety of Chinese greens when you feel comfortable with these basic recipes.

Daikon and Vermicelli Soup

Easy to prepare and rewarding to serve.

½ lb.	daikon*	250 g
1 tsp.	finely chopped ginger root	5 mL
1 tbsp.	finely chopped green onion	15 mL
1 tsp.	vegetable oil	5 mL
1 tsp.	soy sauce	5 mL
2 cups	water	500 mL
3½ oz.	vermicelli**	100 g
½ tsp.	salt	2 mL
¼ cup	peeled shrimp	50 mL
¼ tsp.	pepper	1 mL

1. Cut daikon into strips.
2. Finely chop ginger and green onion.
3. Heat vegetable oil in a large frying pan or wok over high heat. Add ginger and soy sauce; cook ½ minute. Add water. (If your frying pan is not big enough use a saucepan.) When water is boiling add daikon, vermicelli, salt and peeled shrimp; cook 2 minutes. When soup boils, turn heat to medium; cook 3 minutes. When vermicelli turns soft, add green onion and pepper. Serve immediately.

Serves 4.

Pictured on page 71

* Daikon is a sweet, fresh-tasting, crisp oriental radish. It can be from 6–12" (15–30 cm) long and 2–3" (5–7 cm) in diameter. Sliced or shredded, it can be used in soups, salads and stir-fries. Icicle radish or white turnip would be the best substitutes.

**Vermicelli is very thin strands of pasta. The strands are much thinner than regular spaghetti.

Pork with Spinach Soup

This may be served as a first course to whet your appetite.

¼ lb.	lean pork	125 g
1 tsp.	soy sauce	5 mL
½ lb.	spinach	250 g
2 cups	water	500 mL
¼ tsp.	salt	1 mL
¼ tsp.	sesame oil	1 mL

1. Cut pork into thin slices ½ x 1" (1.3 x 2.5 cm). Combine with soy sauce in a bowl.
2. Cut spinach into 2" (5 cm) long pieces.
3. Bring water to a boil in a saucepan over high heat. Lower heat to medium. Add pork; cook 3 minutes. When pork turns white, add spinach and salt. When soup is boiling again, add the sesame oil.

Serves 4.

Pictured on page 53

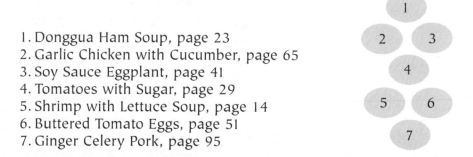

Pork with Cucumber Soup

This quick and healthy soup goes well with fried rice.

¼ lb.	lean pork	125 g
1 tsp.	soy sauce	5 mL
¼ tsp.	ginger powder	1 mL
½ cup	English cucumber slices	125 mL
1 tbsp.	finely chopped green onion	15 mL
2 cups	water	500 mL
¼ tsp.	salt	1 mL
¼ tsp.	sesame oil	1 mL

1. Cut pork into thin slices ½ x 1" (1.3 x 2.5 cm). Mix with soy sauce and ginger powder in a bowl.
2. Cut cucumber into slices. Chop green onion.
3. Bring water to a boil in a saucepan over high heat. Lower heat to medium. Add pork; cook 3 minutes. When pork turns white add cucumber and salt; cook 1 minute. Add green onion and sesame oil. Serve immediately.

Serves 4.

Pictured on page 35

1	2
3	4
5	6
7	8

1. Egg Custard with Green Onion, page 50
2. Garlic Fried Potatoes, page 42
3. Garlic Beef with Broccoli, page 82
4. Peanut Butter Noodles, page 49
5. Green Onion Shrimp with Tofu, page 60
6. Green Onion Garlic Beef, page 78
7. Garlic Daikon, page 34
8. Tomato Egg Soup, page 26

Won Ton Cucumber Soup

This delicious and traditional soup pleases every guest.

Won Tons

1 tsp.	chopped ginger	5 mL
¼ lb.	ground pork	125 g
1 tsp.	soy sauce	5 mL
20	won ton wrappers	20

Soup

½ cup	cucumber slices	125 mL
1 tbsp.	chopped green onion	15 mL
2 cups	water	500 mL
½ cup	cold water	125 mL
½ cup	chicken stock (optional)	125 mL
	see chicken broth on page 12	
¼ tsp.	salt	1 mL
¼ tsp.	sesame oil	1 mL

Won Tons:

1. Chop ginger into small pieces.
2. To make won ton filling, mix ground pork with soy sauce and ginger in a bowl.
3. To make won tons:

   (1) Put ½ tsp. (2 mL) filling just off-center on a wrapper.

   (2) Roll A corner to the center.

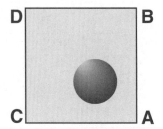

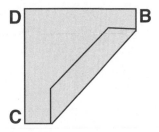

Won Ton Cucumber Soup *continued on next page.*

Won Ton Cucumber Soup *continued*

(3) Fold B and dab a little water on C corner.

(4) Fold the C corner over the B corner. Press together.

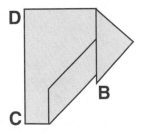 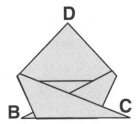 

Soup:

4. Cut cucumber into slices and chop green onion into small pieces.
5. Bring 2 cups (500 mL) of water to a boil in a saucepan over high heat; add won tons. When the water boils again, add cold water. When the won tons float on the water, add cucumber, chicken stock and salt. When the soup is boiling again, add green onion and sesame oil. Serve immediately.

Serves 4.

Pictured on page 54

Won Tons

These bite-sized Chinese dumplings may be filled with meat, sea-food or vegetables mixtures. Try them in other soup recipes, and also try substituting finely chopped cooked shrimp for the ground pork. Won Ton skins are available in many supermarkets. Filled won tons are often deep-fried* and served as appetizers with sweet or spicy dipping sauces. They may also be boiled or steamed.

* **Deep-Fried Won Tons:** Heat 1 cup (250 mL) vegetable oil in a sauce-pan or wok over high heat;** deep-fry won ton in small batches. When won ton turns golden brown remove it from the oil and drain.

**See note on deep-fat frying on page 56.

Meatball Cucumber Soup

This soup tastes wonderful with any stir-fry dish.

1 tbsp.	finely chopped green onion	15 mL
½ lb.	cucumber	250 g
½ lb.	ground pork	250 g
¼ tsp.	ginger powder	1 mL
½ tsp.	salt	2 mL
1 tbsp.	cornstarch	15 mL
2 cups	water	500 mL
¼ tsp.	sesame oil	1 mL
¼ tsp.	pepper	1 mL

1. Finely chop green onion.
2. Cut cucumber into thin slices.
3. Mix ground pork with green onion, ginger powder, ¼ tsp. (1 mL) salt, and cornstarch. Make 1" (2.5 cm) meatballs.
4. Bring water to a boil in a saucepan over high heat. Lower heat to medium. Add meatballs; cook 4 minutes. When meatballs are floating on the water, add cucumber and remaining salt. Cook 3 minutes. Add sesame oil and pepper. Serve immediately.

Serves 4.

Pictured on page 72

Cucumber

If you use firm English cucumbers, peeling is not necessary. If you use other varieties, peel and seed the cucumbers before using.

Chinese cooking uses cucumbers both raw and cooked. A wide variety of pickled and preserved raw cucumber dishes are popular throughout China. For cooking, some Chinese recipes use matured, golden-colored cucumbers, and other recipes use green cucumbers in soups, stir-fries and steamed dishes.

Donggua Ham Soup

Serve this with toasted bread.

½ lb.	donggua*	250 g
¼ cup	chopped ham	60 mL
1 tbsp.	finely chopped onion	15 mL
1 tsp.	vegetable oil	5 mL
¼ tsp.	salt	1 mL
2 cups	water	500 mL
¼ tsp.	pepper	1 mL

1. Cut donggua into 1½" (4 cm) long slices.
2. Cut ham into 1" (2.5 cm) long slices. Finely chop onion.
3. Heat vegetable oil in a frying pan or wok over high heat. Add onion and stir-fry for ½ minute. When you smell the onion, add donggua and salt; stir-fry 3 minutes. (If your frying pan is not large enough, use a saucepan.) Add water and ham. When water is boiling, turn heat to medium; cook 2 minutes. Add the pepper.

Serves 4.

Pictured on page 17

* Donggua is a winter melon or white gourd. The skin is green and the pulp is white in color. Cut off all of the green skin and scoop out the center fibers and seeds. Substitute English cucumber if donggua is not available.

Donggua or Don Gua (Winter Melon)

This vegetable looks like a pumpkin, and can grow as large as a pumpkin. Usually steamed, boiled, or poached in a soup, the cooked flesh is sweet and translucent. Chinese people have long used donggua as a diuretic, and as a cough preventative. It was also recommended for people who wanted to lose weight.

Spinach Egg Noodle Soup

Chinese soups are often enjoyed throughout a meal or served after the main part of the meal.

¼ lb.	spinach	125 g
1 tbsp.	finely chopped green onion	15 mL
3 cups	water	750 mL
3 oz.	pkg. instant oriental noodles*	85 g
1	egg	1
1 tsp.	soy sauce	5 mL
¼ tsp.	salt	1 mL
¼ tsp.	sesame oil	1 mL

1. Cut spinach into 2" (5 cm) strips.
2. Finely chop green onion.
3. Bring water to a boil in a saucepan over high heat. Add noodles and cook 3 minutes. When noodles soften, add whole egg carefully and simmer until egg is set. If you prefer the egg in threads throughout the soup, slowly pour in beaten egg. Stir gently in 1 direction. Cook 1 minute. Add spinach, soy sauce and salt; mix well. Cook 2 minutes. Add green onion and sesame oil.

Serves 1–2.

Pictured on page 36

Variation: to make Spinach Noodle Soup, simply omit the egg.

* The instant oriental noodles used here are available in most supermarkets. They are often packaged as soups with a foil pouch of flavoring. See notes on noodles on page 46. Other types of noodles may be substituted for instant noodles.

Cream of Corn Egg Soup

A healthy and delicious soup for anytime. *

1	egg	1
1 tbsp.	cornstarch	15 mL
2 tbsp.	water	30 mL
2 cups	water	500 mL
14 oz.	can cream-style corn	398 mL
¼ tsp.	salt	1 mL

1. In a bowl, beat egg well.
2. Mix cornstarch with water in a separate bowl.
3. Bring 2 cups (500 mL) of water to a boil in a saucepan over high heat. Add cream-style corn; mix well. When corn boils, turn heat to medium, add cornstarch and mix well. Cook 2 minutes. Slowly pour in beaten egg. Stir gently in 1 direction. Add salt.

Serves 4.

Pictured on page 36

* When my grandmother cooked this dish, she added some sesame oil. When I was a child, I preferred to add some sugar instead of the salt. You can try both variations to see which you prefer.

Tomato Egg Soup

A colorful and tasty soup for a light meal.

2	medium tomatoes	2
1	egg	1
1 tbsp.	finely chopped onion	15 mL
1 tbsp.	cornstarch	15 mL
2 tbsp.	water	30 mL
1 tbsp.	vegetable oil	15 mL
1 tsp.	soy sauce	5 mL
½ tsp.	salt	2 mL
½ tsp.	sugar	2 mL
2 cups	boiling water	500 mL

1. Cut tomatoes into pieces.
2. In a bowl, beat egg well.
3. Finely chop onion.
4. Mix cornstarch with water in another bowl.
5. Heat vegetable oil in a frying pan or wok over high heat. Add onion and stir-fry for ½ minute. When you can smell the onion, add tomato, soy sauce, salt and sugar. Stir-fry for 2 minutes. When tomato turns soft, add boiling water. (If your frying pan is not big enough, use a saucepan.) Add cornstarch; mix well. When the soup is boiling again, slowly pour in the beaten egg. Stir gently in 1 direction.

Serves 4.

Pictured on page 18

Chili and Sour Soup

A great soup for a cold winter day.

12 oz.	pkg. tofu	350 g
½	medium carrot, chopped	½
½	green onion, chopped	½
1	egg	1
1 tbsp.	cornstarch	15 mL
2 tbsp.	water	30 mL
2 cups	water	500 mL
2 tbsp.	peas	30 mL
1 tbsp.	soy sauce	15 mL
¼ tsp.	salt	1 mL
1 tsp.	vinegar	5 mL
½ tsp.	hot chili powder*	2 mL
	or Garlic, Chili and Onion Sauce, page 29	
¼ tsp.	sesame oil	1 mL
¼ tsp.	pepper	1 mL

1. Cut tofu into pieces ½ x 1" (1.3 x 2.5 cm).
2. Finely chop carrot and green onion.
3. In a bowl, beat egg well.
4. Mix cornstarch with water in another bowl.
5. Bring 2 cups (500 mL) of water to a boil in a saucepan over high heat. Add tofu, carrot, peas, soy sauce, salt, vinegar and hot chili powder; mix well. When soup boils, turn heat to low; cook 3 minutes. Add cornstarch, mix well, cook 2 minutes. Slowly pour in beaten egg. Stir gently in 1 direction. Stir in green onion, sesame oil and pepper. Serve immediately.

Serves 6. Pictured on page 72

* Chinese or Asian chili powder is very different from North American or Mexican Chili powder. It is more similar to cayenne pepper. Dried red chili flakes are also used in many Chinese dishes. Chile powder or Chili flakes from Chinese markets are usually more pungent than cayenne or hot chili powders from supermarkets. Look for Chinese or Thai brands.

Salads and Condiments

Garlic Vinegar Cucumber

This fresh tangy cucumber salad is a good complement to Chinese dishes.

1 lb.	cucumber	500 g
1	garlic clove	1
¼ tsp.	salt	1 mL
1 tsp.	soy sauce	5 mL
½ tsp.	vinegar	2 mL
¼ tsp.	sesame oil	1 mL

1. Cut cucumber into 1" (2.5 cm) cubes. Chop garlic into small pieces.
2. Mix cucumber with remaining ingredients.

Serves 4. Pictured on page 72

Pickles

Chinese pickles are usually prepared as needed, without a long curing process. Cucumbers, carrots, sweet and hot red peppers, radishes, papaya, etc. are often pickled as snacks or side dishes. Cucumber pickles are sometimes quickly stir-fried, enhanced with a soy vinegar sauce and then chilled before serving. Often crushed red pepper flakes are added.

Tomatoes with Sugar

In this dish, the sugar brings out the full flavor of the tomato.

| 2 | medium tomatoes | 2 |
| 1 tbsp. | sugar* | 15 mL |

1. Cut tomato into wedges. Arrange in a dish.
2. Sprinkle with sugar.

Serves 4. Pictured on page 17

* Sugar is often used as a flavor enhancer in Chinese cooking. It brings out the essential flavor of vegetables and spices without adding obvious sweetness.

Garlic, Chili and Onion Sauce

Use this spicy sauce as a condiment or use it to replace hot chili powder in cooking.

2	minced garlic cloves	2
1 tbsp.	minced onion	15 mL
1 tbsp.	crushed chilies	15 mL
½ tsp.	salt	2 mL
2 tbsp.	vegetable oil	30 mL

1. Mince garlic and onion.
2. In a bowl, combine garlic, onion, chili and salt.
3. Heat oil in a small pan over medium heat. When oil is hot, about 375°F (190°C), turn off heat, add all ingredients and stir-fry for 1 minute. Makes about 5 tbsp. (75 mL) of sauce.

Serves 4.

* Double recipe if you like, cover and store unrefrigerated.

Pickled Garlic – Sour

This sour version seems to appeal more to the North American palate.

¼ lb.	peeled garlic cloves (2 or 3 heads)	100 g
1 ½ cups	vinegar	375 mL

1. Put the garlic cloves in a jar.
2. Add vinegar to the jar and seal.
3. Serve after 2 weeks.

Pickled Garlic – Sweet

Pickled garlic is used in China as a condiment and also as preventative for colds. Children especially like this sweet version.

6 tbsp.	brown sugar	90 mL
½ tsp.	salt	2 mL
½ cup	boiling water	125 mL
2 tbsp.	vinegar	30 mL
¼ lb.	peeled garlic cloves (2 or 3 heads)	100 g

1. In a bowl, combine sugar, salt, water and vinegar; cool.
2. Put the garlic cloves in a clean jar.
3. Pour cold sugar solution into the jar and seal.
4. Serve after 2 weeks.

Pickled Garlic – Sweet and Sour

Sweet and Sour Pickled Garlic is a traditional New Year's dish. For the Chinese Spring Festival, it is served with Chinese dumplings.

¼ lb.	peeled garlic cloves (2 or 3 heads)	100 g
½ cup	rice vinegar	125 mL
1 tbsp.	sugar	15 mL
½ cup	cold water	125 mL

1. In a jar, combine the rice vinegar, sugar and cold water.
2. Add garlic cloves to the jar and seal.
3. Serve after 2 weeks.

Vegetables

Oyster Sauce Mushrooms with Broccoli

Serve this with rice or bread for a light meal.

½ lb.	broccoli	250 g
1	garlic clove	1
1 tsp.	cornstarch	5 mL
¼ tsp.	salt	1 mL
1 tsp.	oyster sauce	5 mL
1 tbsp.	water	15 mL
2 cups.	water	500 mL
1 tbsp.	vegetable oil	15 mL
1 cup	small whole mushrooms*	250 mL

1. Cut broccoli into bite-sized pieces. Finely chop garlic.
2. In a bowl, combine cornstarch, salt, oyster sauce and water to make the sauce.
3. Bring 2 cups (500 mL) of water to a boil in a saucepan over high heat. Add broccoli, cook 2 minutes and drain.
4. Heat oil in a frying pan or wok over high heat; add garlic, mushrooms and broccoli; stir-fry for 2 minutes. Add sauce, stir well and cook 2 minutes.

Serves 4. Pictured on page 72

* Halve or quarter large mushrooms. If you don't have fresh mushrooms, use a 10 oz. (284 mL) can of whole mushrooms. Canned mushrooms add a golden color to this dish.

Variation: Try this delicious oyster sauce with a variety of vegetables. Add sweet peppers, onions, carrots, cauliflower, etc., whatever you have available.

Stir-Fried Vegetables

Try a combination of your favorite vegetables in this simple stir-fry.

½ lb.	broccoli	250 g
2 tbsp.	chopped onion	30 mL
¼ cup	sliced mushrooms	60 mL
1	carrot	1
1	garlic clove	1
½ tsp.	salt	2 mL
1 tsp.	sugar	5 mL
1 tsp.	soy sauce	5 mL
1 tsp.	cornstarch	5 mL
1 tbsp.	water	15 mL
3 cups	water	750 mL
1 tbsp.	vegetable oil	15 mL
½ tsp.	sesame oil	2 mL

1. Cut broccoli into bite-sized pieces. Chop onion and slice mushrooms.
2. Cut carrot into diagonal slices. Mince garlic.
3. In a bowl, combine salt, sugar, soy sauce, cornstarch and 1 tbsp. (15 mL) of water to make the sauce.
4. Bring 2 cups (500 mL) of water to a boil in a saucepan over high heat. Add all vegetables to boiling water; cook for 2 minutes. Drain.
5. Heat vegetable oil in a frying pan or wok over high heat; add garlic and all vegetables. Stir-fry 2 minutes, then add sauce and mix well. When sauce is boiling, cook about 1 minute. Splash on the sesame oil.

Serves 4.

Pictured on page 54

Garlic Gai Lon (Gailan)

This side dish goes with any meat dish.

1 lb.	gai lon*	500 g
1	garlic clove	1
1 tbsp.	vegetable oil	15 mL
1 tsp.	chopped ginger root	5 mL
¼ tsp.	salt	1 mL
1 tbsp.	water	15 mL
½ tsp.	sugar	2 mL

1. Cut gai lon into 2" (5 cm) long strips.
2. Mince garlic.
3. Heat vegetable oil in a frying pan or wok over high heat; add ginger and garlic; stir-fry for ½ minute, until the aroma is released. Add gai lon, salt, water and sugar; stir-fry for 3 minutes.

Serves 4.

Pictured on page 36

* Gai Lon is also known as Chinese broccoli. It is much more leafy, with smaller florets, than regular broccoli. If gai lon is not available in the supermarket, substitute spinach and cook for 1-2 minutes.

Ginger

Fresh ginger, readily available in supermarkets, is an essential part of Chinese cuisine. The aroma is spicy and pungent and the flavor is peppery with a hint of sweetness. Fresh ginger is used grated, slivered and ground. It is not necessary to peel very fresh young ginger before using. See note on ginger storage on page 8. Ginger is also used dried and ground in soups and sweets. Candied or crystallized ginger, preserved in sugar, makes a delicious tangy sweet treat; while pickled ginger, preserved in sweet vinegar, makes a spicy tangy sweet and sour garnish.

Garlic Daikon

You can add meat to this dish to create a more substantial variation.

1 lb.	daikon*	500 g
1	green onion	1
1 tbsp.	vegetable oil	15 mL
¼ tsp.	salt	1 mL
1 tsp.	soy sauce	5 mL

1. Cut daikon into strips. Finely chop green onion.
2. Heat oil in a frying pan or wok over medium heat and add onion. Stir until the onion aroma is evident. Add daikon and stir-fry for 3 minutes. Add salt and soy sauce; stir well. Cook 1 minute.

Serves 4.

Pictured on page 18

* See note on daikon (oriental radish) on page 15.

Sweet and Sour Cabbage

A practical easy-to-cook vegetable dish for lovers of sweet and sour.

1 lb.	cabbage	500 g
2 tbsp.	chopped onion	30 mL
1	garlic clove	1
½ tsp.	salt	2 mL
1 tsp.	sugar	5 mL
1 tsp.	soy sauce	5 mL
1 tsp.	vinegar	5 mL
1 tsp.	cornstarch	5 mL
1 tbsp.	water	15 mL
1 tbsp.	vegetable oil	15 mL

1. Cut cabbage into pieces about 1½" (4 cm).
2. Finely chop onion and garlic.
3. In a bowl, combine salt, sugar, soy sauce, garlic, vinegar, cornstarch and water to make the sauce.
4. Heat vegetable oil in a frying pan or wok over high heat; add onion and stir-fry for ½ minute. When mixture becomes aromatic, add cabbage and stir-fry 3 minutes. When cabbage becomes soft, add sauce and mix well. Cook 2 minutes.

Serves 4.

Pictured on page 35

1	2
3	4
5	6
7	8

1. Cream of Corn Egg Soup, page 25
2. Onion Green Beans with Pork, page 92
3. Yang Zhou Fried Rice, page 43
4. Garlic Gai Lon, page 33
5. Deep-Fried Garlic Ribs, page 97
6. Garlic Chili Sauce with Chicken, page 66
7. Spinach Egg Noodle Soup, page 24
8. Cabbage with Onion and Vinegar, page 38

Cabbage with Onion and Vinegar

This healthy dish is quick and flavorful

1 lb.	cabbage	500 g
2 tbsp.	chopped onion	30 mL
1 tbsp.	vegetable oil	15 mL
1 tbsp.	water (optional)	15 mL
½ tsp.	salt	2 mL
¼ tsp.	vinegar	1 mL

1. Slice cabbage into 1" (2.5 cm) strips.
2. Finely chop onion.
3. Heat vegetable oil in a frying pan or wok over high heat; add onion and stir-fry for 1 minute. Add cabbage and stir-fry about 3 minutes. Add 1 tbsp. (15 mL) of water if you want to make the cabbage softer. Add salt and vinegar; mix well. Cook for 2 minutes.

Serves 4.

Pictured on page 36

Chinese Cabbage

Many varieties of Chinese cabbage are available in North American supermarkets. One of the most commonly used varieties is bok choy, also called Chinese White cabbage, white mustard cabbage, or cole. In appearance it is oval, about 8" (20 cm) long and has broad ribs with thin crinkly leaves. The firm, white, heads have a fresh and delicate flavor. Used in stir-fries and also in soups, it cooks in about 2 minutes.

Cauliflower with Tomato Sauce

Fresh and tasty.

1 lb.	cauliflower	500 g
1 tbsp.	chopped onion	15 mL
¼ tsp.	salt	1 mL
1 tsp.	sugar	5 mL
1 tsp.	soy sauce	5 mL
2 tbsp.	tomato sauce	30 mL
1 tsp.	cornstarch	5 mL
1 tbsp.	water	15 mL
2 cups	water	500 mL
1 tbsp.	vegetable oil	15 mL

1. Cut cauliflower into bite-sized pieces.
2. Finely chop onion.
3. In a bowl, combine salt, sugar, soy sauce, tomato sauce, cornstarch and water to make the sauce.
4. Bring 2 cups (500 mL) of water to a boil in a saucepan over high heat. Add cauliflower to boiling water; cook for 2 minutes. Drain.
5. Heat vegetable oil in a frying pan or wok over high heat, add onion, stir-fry for ½ minute. When the onion aroma is evident, add the sauce and mix well. When the sauce is boiling and becomes clear and red, add cauliflower and stir-fry for 1 minute.

Serves 4.

Pictured on page 71

Sweet and Sour Bean Sprouts

A light and healthy dish.

3 cups	water	750 mL
1 lb.	bean sprouts	500 g
1	green onion	1
1 tbsp.	vegetable oil	15 mL
¼ tsp.	salt	1 mL
1 tsp.	sugar	5 mL
¼ tsp.	vinegar	1 mL

1. Bring water to a boil in a saucepan over high heat. Add bean sprouts and cook for 2 minutes. Drain.
2. Finely chop green onion.
3. Heat vegetable oil in a frying pan or wok over high heat. Add green onion and bean sprouts; stir-fry for 1 minute. Add remaining ingredients. Stir well and cook for 2 minutes.

Serves 4.

Pictured on page 54

Bean Sprouts

Mung bean sprouts are white and gold, crisp tender sprouts from dried green mung beans. The traditional sprouts used in Chinese cooking, they should be cooked very briefly to keep the characteristic crispness. If you are not using them immediately, blanch sprouts in boiling water for 30 seconds. Plunge them into ice water and refrigerate for 2-3 days. Change the water each day.

Soy Sauce Eggplant

Eggplant is very popular in Chinese cooking. This stir-fry version is very tasty.

1 lb.	eggplant	500 g
1 tbsp.	chopped green onion	15 mL
1	garlic clove	1
2 tbsp.	vegetable oil	30 mL
1 tsp.	sugar	5 mL
¼ tsp.	salt	1 mL
1 tbsp.	soy sauce	15 mL
¼ cup	water	60 mL

1. Cut eggplant into 2" (5 cm) long strips.
2. Finely chop green onion and garlic.
3. Heat oil in a frying pan or wok over high heat. Add onion and stir-fry about ½ minute. When the onion aroma is evident, add eggplant; stir-fry for 3 minutes. Add sugar, salt and soy sauce; mix well. Add water. When water has evaporated, add the garlic and mix well.

Serves 4.

Pictured on page 17

Eggplant

Grown in China for over a thousand years, Chinese eggplant, or aubergine, is usually long and slender in shape. Most Chinese eggplant does not need to be peeled. The color varies from deep to light purple and from light green to white. Some eggplant have the appearance of eggs, they are small, round and a pale greenish white. The flesh is slightly sweet tasting and may be stir-fried, baked, steamed, deep-fried, etc. Dark eggplant is usually peeled before cooking. Chinese eggplant does not need to be salted before cooking.

Garlic Fried Potatoes

In northern China, potatoes are one of the main sources of food in the winter. Almost every Chinese family cooks this delicious garlicy potato dish.

2	large potatoes	2
1 tsp.	soy sauce	5 mL
¼ tsp.	salt	1 mL
1 tsp.	sugar	5 mL
½ tsp.	vinegar	2 mL
1	garlic clove, minced	1
1 tbsp.	cold water	15 mL
1 tbsp.	vegetable oil	15 mL
1 tbsp.	minced onion	15 mL

1. Cut potatoes into shoestring or matchstick size.
2. In a bowl, combine soy sauce, salt, sugar, vinegar, garlic and cold water to make the sauce.
3. Heat oil in a frying pan or wok over high heat, add onion, stir for ½ minute. Add potatoes and stir-fry for 3 minutes. Add sauce; mix well. Stir for 3 minutes.

Serves 4. Pictured on page 18

Hot Chili Potatoes

This dish is supposed to be very crunchy when it's done. Don't overcook the potatoes.

1 lb.	potatoes	500 g
2 cups	water	500 mL
½ tsp.	salt	2 mL
1 tsp.	hot chili sauce (Asian), or	5 mL
	Garlic, Chili and Onion Sauce page 29	

1. Cut potatoes into shoestring or matchstick size.
2. Bring water to a boil in a saucepan over high heat. Add potatoes and cook for 3 minutes. Rinse in cold water. Drain.
3. Mix the potatoes well with salt and hot chili sauce.

Serves 4. Pictured on page 72

Yang Zhou Fried Rice

A delicious fried rice with colorful morsels of shrimp, ham and vegetables.

2 tbsp.	chopped shrimp	30 mL
½ tsp.	cornstarch	2 mL
¼ tsp.	pepper	1 mL
2 tbsp.	diced ham	30 mL
1	egg	1
3 tbsp.	vegetable oil	45 mL
2 tbsp.	finely chopped onion	30 mL
2 tbsp.	peas	30 mL
2 cups	cooked rice (page 11)	500 mL
½ tsp.	salt	2 mL
½ cup	water	125 mL
1 tsp.	soy sauce	5 mL
¼ tsp.	sesame oil (optional)	1 mL

1. Mix shrimp with cornstarch and pepper in a small bowl.
2. Dice ham into small cubes. Beat egg well.
3. Heat 1 tbsp. (15 mL) oil in a frying pan or wok over high heat; add beaten egg. When egg begins to set, remove from pan and set aside.
4. Heat remaining oil over medium heat. Add shrimp and stir for 2 minutes. Add onion, ham, peas, eggs, rice and salt. Mix well. Add ½ cup (125 mL) water. When water evaporates, add soy sauce and sesame oil; mix well.

Serves 4. Pictured on page 36

Peas and Rice with Chicken

This quick and easy dish is a complete meal in one bowl.

½ lb.	boneless chicken breasts	250 g
1 tsp.	cornstarch	5 mL
¼ tsp.	salt	1 mL
1 tbsp.	chopped onion	15 mL
2	eggs	2
3 tbsp.	vegetable oil	45 mL
2 tbsp.	peas	30 mL
¼ tsp.	salt	1 mL
2 cups	cooked rice (page 11)	500 mL
½ cup	water	125 mL
¼ tsp.	sesame oil (optional)	1 mL

1. Cut chicken breasts into thin strips. In a bowl, mix chicken with cornstarch and ¼ tsp. (1 mL) salt.
2. Finely chop onion.
3. In another bowl, beat eggs well.
4. Heat 1 tbsp. (15 mL) vegetable oil in a frying pan or wok over high heat; add beaten egg. When egg begins to set, remove from pan and set aside.
5. Heat remaining 2 tbsp. (30 mL) vegetable oil, add chicken and stir-fry for 2 minutes, until meat turns white. Add onion, peas, eggs, salt and rice; mix well. Add ½ cup (125 mL) water. Stir for 2 minutes over low heat. Add sesame oil.

Serves 4.

Pictured on page 35

Noodles

Chinese Cold Noodles

This is a refreshing dish in the summer.

2 tbsp.	chopped ham	30 mL
¼ lb.	cucumber	125 g
1	garlic clove, minced	1
3 oz.	pkg. instant oriental noodles*	85 g
3 cups	water	750 mL
1 tbsp.	chopped onion	15 mL
1 tsp.	soy sauce	5 mL
1 tbsp.	sesame oil	15 mL
½ tsp.	sugar	2 mL
½ tsp.	vinegar	2 mL
½ tsp.	Garlic, Chili and Onion	2 mL
	Sauce, page 29 (optional)	

1. Cut ham and cucumber into 1" (2.5 cm) long shoestring or matchstick shapes.
2. Bring water to a boil in a saucepan over high heat. Add the noodles and lower heat to medium. Cook 3 minutes. When noodles become soft, rinse in cold water and drain.
3. Mix all ingredients together. Refrigerate and serve cold or serve immediately.

Serves 2. Pictured on page 53

* See note about noodles on pages 46 and 47.

Chow Mein (Fresh Steamed Noodles)

Quick and easy, noodle dishes can be a complete meal in one bowl.

4 oz.	chow mein (thin fresh wheat noodles)	113 g
4 cups	water	1 L
1 cup	cold water	250 mL

In a medium saucepan, bring 4 cups (1 L) of water to a boil over high heat. Add noodles; cook 2 minutes. When water is boiling again, add cold water and lower heat to medium; cook 3 minutes. When the noodles are soft, rinse in cold water and drain. Serves 3–4.

Try these noodles in various noodle dishes:
   a. Chinese Cold Noodles, page 45.
   b. Oriental Pork Noodles, page 48.
   c. If you mix these noodles with Celery Chili Beef, page 80, you will have Spicy Noodles.
   d. If you mix these noodles with Stir-Fried Vegetables, page 32, you will have Vegetable Noodles.

Noodles

For centuries noodles have been very popular in China. In addition to the wheat-flour noodles of western cuisine, with or without eggs, Chinese noodles are also made from rice and mung-bean starch. There is even a special very long noodle, called long life noodle, served on birthdays. As with pasta, in most recipes, the noodles can be readily substituted for one another. Also, if you don't have Chinese noodles on hand, pasta of a similar shape and size may be substituted.

Wheat Flour Noodles (Lo-Mein)

Available in various widths, some as thin as vermicelli, some as thick as $1/4$" (1 cm) e.g. the yellow Shanghai or miki noodles, these noodles are available fresh or dried and some are made with eggs. Fresh noodles cook in 2-3 minutes; dry noodles cook in 7-10 minutes. After cooking, drain and rinse noodles. Use immediately in soups or stir-fries, or, if using in a cold salad, toss drained noodles with 1 tbsp. (15 mL) of sesame oil and sprinkle with salt. Refrigerate in an airtight container up to 2 days. Cook fresh

Chinese egg noodles as you would spaghetti or similar-shaped pasta. Cooked, drained egg noodles may be dried on a towel and then deep-fried. Commercial chow mein noodles are western adaptations of crispy deep-fried noodles. **Chaomian**, a soft fried noodle, is more authentic. **Mein sein** are very fine wheat noodles. They need only a few seconds immersion in boiling soup and they are ready to eat. Substitute linguine, spaghetti, fettuccine.

Bean Thread Noodles (Fensi, Fun-See, Fen Szu, Sai Fun)

Translucent and very thin, these dry noodles, made from mung bean starch, are called cellophane noodles, glass noodles, silver noodles, Chinese Vermicelli and jelly noodles. With scissors, cut the amount of noodles you want from the folded skein, if not using the whole skein. Soak the noodles in very hot water for about 20-30 seconds, until they are softened to the desired consistency. Noodles for stir-fry recipes should be firmer than noodles for soups. Drain noodles and use immediately in soups or stir-fries. Cook no more than 3 minutes or they will become mushy. These noodles absorb a lot of liquid and although they have little flavor of their own, they absorb the flavors of the cooking liquid. Dry bean threads can be cut into lengths for deep frying. Fry at 400°F (200°C) just until puffed and golden. Soaked, drained bean threads may be refrigerated for up to 3 days. Resoak in warm water before use, if necesary. Substitute vermicelli.

Rice Stick Noodles (Mee-Fun, My-Foon, Ngunsi-Fun, Lai-Fun)

Opaque, dry white wavy noodles made from rice flour, these are also called Chinese vermicelli. Soak in cold water just until soft and use in soups and stir-fries. Cook for 2-3 minutes. Dry rice sticks may be deep-fried as the bean thread noodles and used as crunchy toppings for salads or vegetable dishes.

Dried Rice Noodles (Ho-Fun)

Similar to rice stick noodles, but wider and often flat. Soak and cook as for rice stick noodles, but increase cooking time to 6-10 minutes.

Fresh Rice Noodles (Look-Fun)

Sold in the refrigeration section of supermarkets, these sheets of soft dough are slightly cooked. Cut sheets into strips or pieces and cook 1-2 minutes in soups or stir-fries. Don't overcook.

Instant Noodles

These noodles are sold in packages, often with flavor packets. Precooked and dried, they are added to soups or sauces and they cook in 3 minutes. Most of these noodles are made from wheat flour.

Oriental Pork Noodles

A simple but delicious noodle dish with many variations.

½ lb.	uncooked lean pork	250 g
1 tsp.	soy sauce	5 mL
1 tsp.	cornstarch	5 mL
3 oz.	pkg. instant oriental noodles	85 g
3 cups	water	750 mL
½	green pepper	½
½	carrot	½
1 tbsp.	chopped onion	15 mL
2 tbsp.	vegetable oil	30 mL
¼ tsp.	salt	1 mL

1. Cut pork roast into 2" (5 cm) long strips. Mix with soy sauce and cornstarch in a bowl.
2. In a medium saucepan, bring water to a boil; turn heat to medium and add noodles; cook 3 minutes. When noodles become soft, rinse in cold water and drain.
3. Cut green pepper and carrot into strips. Finely chop onion.
4. Heat vegetable oil in frying pan or wok over high heat; add pork and stir-fry for 2 minutes. Add onion, salt, green pepper and carrot; stir well. Cook for 2 minutes. Add noodles and mix well.

Serves 4.

Pictured on page 71

Variations: Make Oriental Beef, Chicken or Shrimp Noodles by substituting beef, chicken or shrimp for the pork. Broccoli, red peppers and/or mushrooms also make delicious additions. Use your imagination and what you have on hand. Also try this dish with the fresh noodles on page 46.

Peanut Butter Noodles

A Chinese way of using peanut butter. This dish was developed in North America.

¼	English cucumber	¼
1	garlic clove	1
3 oz.	pkg. instant oriental noodles	85 g
3 cups	water	750 mL
1 tbsp.	warm water	15 mL
¼ tsp.	salt	1 mL
1 tbsp.	peanut butter	15 mL
½ tsp.	vinegar	2 mL

1. Cut cucumber into diagonal slices and cut slices into shoestring or matchstick shapes.
2. Mince or crush garlic.
3. In a medium saucepan, bring 3 cups (750 mL) of water to a boil, turn heat to medium and add noodles; cook 3 minutes. When noodles become soft, rinse in cold water and drain.
4. To make sauce, combine 1 tbsp. (15 mL) warm water, salt and peanut butter.
5. Add cucumber, garlic, vinegar and peanut sauce to the noodles and mix well.

Serves 4.

Pictured on page 18

Variation: Try this dish with any of the fresh noodles or rice noodles on pages 46 and 47. Also, if you like spicy food, add crushed red pepper flakes or the Garlic, Chili and Onion Sauce on page 29, to taste.

Eggs

Egg Custard with Green Onion

This savory and nutritious custard is served in Chinese homes for breakfast or lunch with steamed bread or toast. It is very popular for young children and also for nursing mothers or people with colds and sore throats.

1	green onion	1
2	eggs	2
¼ tsp.	salt	1 mL
½ cup	water	125 mL
½ tsp.	soy sauce	2 mL
½ tsp.	sesame oil	2 mL

1. Finely chop green onion.
2. Beat eggs in a microwave-safe bowl. Add salt, green onion and water; mix well. Cook in a microwave, covered, for 2-3 minutes on high.
3. Stir in soy sauce and sesame oil.

Serves 1 or 2.

Pictured on page 18

Buttered Tomato Eggs

A combination of Western and Oriental favors.

4	eggs	4
1 tbsp.	chopped onion	15 mL
2	medium tomatoes, diced	2
2 tbsp.	vegetable oil	30 mL
1 tsp.	butter	5 mL
¼ tsp.	salt	1 mL
1 tsp.	sugar	5 mL
1 tsp.	soy sauce	5 mL

1. In a bowl, beat eggs well.
2. Finely chop onion. Dice tomato.
3. Heat 1 tbsp. (30 mL) oil in frying pan or wok over high heat, pour in beaten eggs. Scramble. When eggs are set, add butter and stir well. Remove from pan; set aside.
4. Heat remaining oil in frying pan or work over high heat. Add tomato and onion; stir-fry for 2 minutes. Add salt, sugar and soy sauce; stir for 2 minutes. When tomato softens, add egg and stir well.

Serves 4.

Pictured on page 17

Variation: To make Buttered Tomato Egg Noodles, add noodles on page 46.

Tomatoes in Chinese Cuisine

Tomatoes are not traditional in Chinese cooking. Green tomatoes were first used as a tart side dish in the early part of the 1900s. However, with the excellent Chinese cooks adopting North American produce to traditional Chinese recipes, the tomato is now being used in soups and stir-fry recipes.

Onion Eggs

This is a basic Chinese dish. Serve with vegetable or meat dishes and rice. Or serve North American style for breakfast. Try it also as a sandwich, between slices of toast.

4	eggs	4
1	medium onion	1
2 tbsp.	vegetable oil	30 mL
½ tsp.	salt	2 mL

1. In a bowl, beat eggs well. Slice onion thinly.
2. Heat oil in a frying pan or wok over high heat. Add beaten eggs. When eggs begin to set, add the onion and salt; mix well. Cook 2 minutes.

Serves 4.

Pictured on page 35

1. Celery Chili Beef, page 80
2. Tomato Pork Cutlets, page 94
3. Black Bean Mushroom Chicken, page 67
4. Green Pepper with Stir-Fried Chicken, page 70
5. Chinese Cold Noodles, page 45
6. Tofu with Oyster Sauce, page 56
7. Fried Lettuce with Beef, page 77
8. Pork with Spinach Soup, page 16

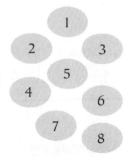

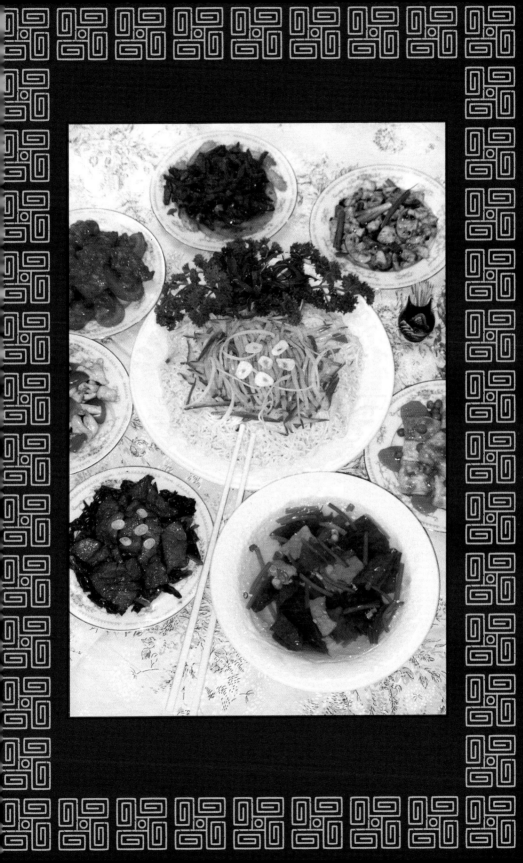

Onion Tofu

Tofu is delicious and healthy. It is usually served daily in Chinese family meals.

12 oz.	pkg. tofu (see note on page 9)	350 g
2	green onions	2
1 tbsp.	vegetable oil	15 mL
½ tsp.	salt	2 mL

1. Cut tofu into ½" (1.3 cm) cubes.
2. Chop green onion into small pieces.
3. Heat vegetable oil in a frying pan or wok over high heat. Add green onion and salt; stir for ½ minute. When the onion aroma is evident add the tofu. Stir-fry for 3 minutes.

Serves 4.

Pictured on page 72

1	2
3	4
5	6
7	8

1. Stir-Fried Vegetables, page 32
2. Sweet and Sour Bean Sprouts, page 40
3. Pork with Egg and Peas, page 88
4. Won Ton Cucumber Soup, page 20
5. Tomato Ginger Chicken, page 74
6. Beef-Fried Cucumber, page 81
7. Green Onion Pork, page 89
8. Soy Sauce Beef with Onion, page 84

Tofu with Oyster Sauce

A beautiful dish for lovers of tofu, it is very easy to digest and very flavorful.

12 oz.	pkg. tofu (see note on page 9)	350 g
1	carrot	1
1 tbsp.	chopped onion	15 mL
1	garlic clove	1
1 tbsp.	oyster sauce	15 mL
½ tsp.	sugar	2 mL
1 tsp.	soy sauce	5 mL
1 tsp.	cornstarch	5 mL
2 tbsp.	water	30 mL
1 cup	vegetable oil	250 mL
2 tbsp.	peas	30 mL

1. Cut tofu into 1" (2.5 cm) cubes.
2. Cut carrot into thin diagonal slices. Finely chop onion and garlic.
3. To make the sauce, combine oyster sauce, sugar, soy sauce, cornstarch, garlic and water.
4. Heat 1 cup (250 mL) vegetable oil in a saucepan or wok over high heat; deep-fry tofu in small batches. When tofu turns golden brown remove it from the oil and drain.
5. Heat 1 tbsp. (15 mL) oil in frying pan or wok over high heat, add onion and carrot and stir-fry for 1 minute. Add tofu and sauce; stir-fry for 2 minutes, or until sauce boils and turns clear.

Serves 4.

Pictured on page 53

Deep-Fried Foods

The average oil temperature for deep-frying is 375°F (190°C) but the temperature does vary for various types of food — a deep-fat thermometer is advised.

Hot Chili Tofu

This hot tofu dish is spicy and hearty. It is perfect for when you are really hungry.

12 oz.	pkg. tofu (see note on page 9)	350 g
1/4 lb.	lean ground beef	125 g
1 tsp.	soy sauce	5 mL
1 tbsp.	chopped onion	15 mL
1 tsp.	chopped ginger root	5 mL
1	garlic clove	1
1 tsp.	sugar	5 mL
1 tsp.	black bean sauce	5 mL
1 tsp.	cornstarch	5 mL
2 tbsp.	water	30 mL
2 tbsp.	vegetable oil	30 mL
1 tsp.	hot chili powder*, or Garlic Chili and Onion Sauce on page 29	5 mL
1/4 tsp.	pepper	1 mL

1. Cut tofu into 1/2" (1.3 cm) cubes.
2. Mix ground beef with soy sauce in a bowl.
3. Finely chop onion, ginger root and garlic.
4. In another bowl, combine sugar, black bean sauce, cornstarch and water to make the sauce.
5. Heat vegetable oil in frying pan or wok over high heat, add ground beef and stir-fry for 3 minutes. When ground beef is crumbly, add onion, ginger, garlic and chili powder; stir-fry for 2 minutes. When mixture becomes aromatic, add tofu and stir-fry for 2 minutes. Add sauce, mix well and cook 3 minutes. Stir in pepper.

Serves 4. Pictured on page 72

* See note on hot chili powder on page 27.

Black Bean Sauce

Fermented black soybeans have a pungent, salty flavor. They are used to make sauces for a variety of meat and fish dishes.

Ginger Beef with Tofu

An excellent choice for a special menu.

½ lb.	uncooked lean beef	250 g
1 tsp.	cornstarch	5 mL
1 tsp.	vegetable oil	5 mL
12 oz.	pkg. tofu (see note on page 9)	350 g
1	green onion	1
1 tsp.	minced ginger root	5 mL
½ tsp.	salt	2 mL
1 tsp.	cornstarch	5 mL
2 tbsp.	water	30 mL
1 cup	vegetable oil	250 mL

1. Cut beef into thin slices, 1 x ½" (2.5 x 1.3 cm). In a bowl, combine 1 tsp. (5 mL) cornstarch and 1 tsp. (5 mL) oil. Stir in beef and set aside.
2. Cut tofu into 1 x 1 x ½" (2.5 x 2.5 x 1.3 cm) pieces.
3. Cut green onion into 2" (5 cm) lengths. Mince ginger.
4. In another bowl, combine salt, cornstarch and water to make a sauce.
5. Heat oil over high heat* in a large saucepan. Deep-fry tofu in small batches. When tofu turns golden brown, remove it from the oil and drain. Repeat until all tofu is deep-fried.
6. Heat 1 tbsp. (15 mL) oil in a frying pan or wok over high heat. Add beef and ginger; stir-fry 2 minutes. When beef turns brown, add tofu and mix well. Add sauce and stir for 2 minutes. Add green onion; mix well.

Serves 4.

Pictured on the back cover

* See note on deep-fat frying on page 56.

Ginger Pork with Tofu

A very good summer family dish.

½ lb.	boneless pork chops	250 g
1 tsp.	soy sauce	5 mL
1 tsp.	cornstarch	5 mL
12 oz.	pkg. tofu (see note on page 9)	350 g
1 tsp.	minced ginger root	5 mL
1	green pepper	1
½ cup	sliced carrots	125 mL
½ tsp.	salt	2 mL
1 tsp.	sugar	5 mL
1 tsp.	cornstarch	5 mL
2 tbsp.	water	30 mL
1 cup	vegetable oil	250 mL
1	green onion, finely chopped	1

1. Cut pork into thin slices 1½ x 1" (4 x 2.5 cm). Mix with soy sauce and 1 tsp. (5 mL) cornstarch in a bowl.
2. Cut tofu into 1½" (4 cm) cubes.
3. Mince ginger. Cut green pepper into 2" (5 cm) long strips. Cut carrot into thin slices.
4. In a bowl, combine salt, sugar, 1 tsp. (5 mL) cornstarch and water to make the sauce.
5. Heat 1 cup (250 mL) vegetable oil in a frying pan or wok over high heat*; deep-fry tofu in small batches. When tofu turns golden brown, remove it from the oil and drain.
6. Heat 1 tbsp. (15 mL) oil in a frying pan or wok over high heat; add ginger and pork slices. Stir-fry for 2 minutes. When pork turns brown add tofu, green pepper and carrot; stir-fry for 2 minutes. Add sauce, stir-fry for 2 minutes. Sprinkle with green onion and mix well.

Serves 4

Pictured on page 71

* See note on deep-fat frying on page 56.

Green Onion Shrimp with Tofu

A colorful dish that everyone likes. It has a fresh and delightful fragrance.

12 oz.	pkg. tofu	350 g
1 tsp.	chopped ginger root	5 mL
1	garlic clove	1
1	green onion	1
¼ cup	peeled shrimp	50 mL
¼ tsp.	pepper	1 mL
1 tsp.	cornstarch	5 mL
½ tsp.	salt	2 mL
1 tsp.	sugar	5 mL
2 tbsp.	water	30 mL
1 tsp.	cornstarch	5 mL
2 cups	vegetable oil	500 mL

1. Cut tofu into 1½" (4 cm) cubes.
2. Finely chop ginger and garlic. Cut green onion into 2" (5 cm) lengths.
3. In a bowl, mix shrimp with pepper and 1 tsp. (5 mL) cornstarch.
4. In another bowl, combine salt, sugar, garlic, water and 1 tsp. (5 mL) cornstarch to make the sauce.
5. Heat vegetable oil in a saucepan over high heat* and deep-fry tofu in small batches. When the tofu turns golden brown remove it from the oil and drain.
6. Heat 1 tbsp. (15 mL) oil in a frying pan or wok over high heat, add ginger and stir for ½ minute. When you smell the ginger, add shrimp; stir-fry about 2 minutes. Add tofu and sauce; stir-fry for 2 minutes. When sauce turns clear, add the green onion and mix well.

Serves 4.

Pictured on page 18

* See note on deep-fat frying on page 56.

Sweet and Sour Fish Fillets

Your friends will ask for this recipe.

½ lb.	fish fillets	250 g
½ tsp.	powdered ginger	2 mL
1	egg, beaten	1
2 tbsp.	cornstarch	30 mL
1 tbsp.	chopped onion	15 mL
1 tbsp.	tomato sauce	15 mL
1 tsp.	sugar	5 mL
1 tsp.	soy sauce	5 mL
1 tsp.	cornstarch	5 mL
2 tbsp.	water	30 mL
2 cups	vegetable oil	500 mL

1. Cut fillets into 2" (5 cm) long pieces. In a bowl, mix ginger powder, egg and 2 tbsp. (30 mL) cornstarch. Stir in fish.
2. Finely chop onion. In another bowl, combine tomato sauce, sugar, soy sauce, 1 tsp. (5 mL) cornstarch and water together to make the sauce.
3. Heat oil in a saucepan over high heat* and deep-fry fish. When fish turns golden brown remove it from the pan and drain it.
4. Heat 1 tsp. (5 mL) oil in a frying pan over medium heat. Stir-fry onion for ½ minute. Add sauce. When sauce is boiling add fish pieces and stir well. Cook 2 minutes.

Serves 4. Pictured on the back cover

* See note on deep-fat frying on page 56.

Ginger Squid With Green Pepper

This wonderful dish is particularly good during the summer.

½ lb.	squid tubes	227 g
½	medium green pepper	½
2 tsp.	chopped ginger root	10 mL
¼ tsp.	salt	1 mL
½ tsp.	sugar	2 mL
1 tsp.	soy sauce	5 mL
1 tsp.	cornstarch	5 mL
1 tbsp.	water	15 mL
1 tbsp.	vegetable oil	15 mL

1. Slit squid tubes to make a flat shape, cut squid into strips.
2. Cut green pepper into strips. Finely chop ginger root.
3. In a bowl, combine salt, sugar, soy sauce, cornstarch and water to make the sauce.
4. Heat vegetable oil in a frying pan or wok over high heat; add ginger and cook ½ minute. Add squid; stir-fry 3 minutes. Add green pepper and stir-fry for 2 minutes. Add sauce; mix well and cook 2 minutes.

Serves 4.

Pictured on page 72

Squid

Both Oriental and Mediterranean cuisines prize the mild sweetish flavor and chewy texture of squid. Available fresh, frozen, pickled, canned and dried, larger supermarkets should have both whole squid and the tubes. Do not overcook squid or it will become rubbery. Fresh squid should have a fresh smell and should be stored covered and refrigerated for only 1 or 2 days.

Chicken with Shrimp and Squid

This tender and flavorful dish will delight all your friends.

½ lb.	chicken breasts	250 g
I tsp.	cornstarch	5 mL
I	squid (about 3½ oz. [100 g])	I
I tsp.	chopped ginger root	5 mL
¼ tsp.	salt	I mL
I tsp.	soy sauce	5 mL
I tsp.	cornstarch	5 mL
2 tbsp.	water	30 mL
3 tbsp.	vegetable oil	45 mL
¼ lb.	peeled shrimp	125 g
2 tbsp.	peas	30 mL
½ tsp.	sesame oil	2 mL

1. Cut chicken breasts into thin slices. Mix with I tsp. (5 mL) cornstarch in a bowl.
2. Cut squid into pieces 2 x I " (5 x 2.5 cm). Finely chop ginger root.
3. In a bowl, combine salt, soy sauce, I tsp. (5 mL) cornstarch and water to make the sauce.
4. Heat oil in a frying pan or wok over high heat. Add chicken and ginger; stir-fry for 2 minutes. Add shrimp and squid; stir-fry for 2 minutes. Add peas and sauce and mix well. Cook 2 minutes. Add sesame oil.

Serves 4. Pictured on the back cover

Chicken Breast with Oyster Sauce

Add some peas and carrots for additional color.

1 lb.	chicken breasts	500 g
¼ tsp.	salt	1 mL
1 tsp.	cornstarch	5 mL
2	green onions	2
1 tsp.	grated ginger root	5 mL
1 tbsp.	oyster sauce	15 mL
1 tsp.	soy sauce	5 mL
1 tbsp.	water	15 mL
2 tbsp.	vegetable oil	30 mL

1. Cut chicken breasts into thin slices. Add salt and cornstarch; mix well.
2. Cut green onion into 2" (5 cm) lengths. Grate ginger root.
3. In a bowl, combine oyster sauce, soy sauce and water to make the sauce.
4. Heat vegetable oil in a frying pan or wok over high heat, add ginger and chicken breast strips; stir-fry for 2 minutes. When chicken turns white, add sauce and mix well; cook 2 minutes. Add green onion and stir-fry for 1 minute.

Serves 4.

Pictured on page 71

Garlic Chicken with Cucumber

Cucumber adds a special fragrance and subtle flavor.

1 lb.	chicken breasts	500 g
1 tsp.	cornstarch	5 mL
1 tsp.	water	5 mL
½ tsp.	ginger powder	2 mL
¼	English cucumber	¼
2 tbsp.	chopped onion	30 mL
1	garlic clove	1
½ tsp.	salt	2 mL
1 tsp.	cornstarch	5 mL
2 tbsp.	water	30 mL
2 tbsp.	vegetable oil	30 mL
1 tsp.	sesame oil*	5 mL

1. Cut chicken breasts into 1" (2.5 cm) squares. In a bowl, combine 1 tsp. (5 mL) cornstarch, 1 tsp. (5 mL) water and ginger powder. Stir in chicken.
2. Cut cucumber into 1" (2.5 cm) cubes. Finely chop onion and the garlic.
3. In another bowl, combine salt, garlic, 1 tsp. (5 mL) cornstarch and 2 tbsp. (30 mL) water to make the sauce.
4. Heat vegetable oil over medium heat in a 12" (30 cm) frying pan or wok. Add onion and diced chicken, and stir-fry for 2 minutes. When chicken turns white, add cucumber and mix well. Add sauce, and stir-fry about 2 minutes. When the sauce boils, add sesame oil.

Serves 4.

Pictured on page 17

* Sesame oil has a very distinctive flavor that many people enjoy. It can be an acquired taste — try it and see.

Garlic Chili Sauce with Chicken

A dish to warm you on a cold winter day.

1 lb.	chicken breasts	500 g
1 tsp.	cornstarch	5 mL
1 tsp.	water	5 mL
2 tbsp.	finely chopped onion	30 mL
1 tsp.	finely chopped ginger root	5 mL
1 tsp.	cornstarch	5 mL
2 tsp.	sugar	10 mL
¼ tsp.	salt	1 mL
1 tbsp.	garlic chili sauce (Asian)*	15 mL
1 tbsp.	soy sauce	15 mL
1 tbsp.	water	15 mL
2 tbsp.	vegetable oil	30 mL
2 tbsp.	cooked blanched peanuts**	30 mL

1. Cut chicken breasts into thin slices. In a bowl, mix 1 tsp. (5 mL) cornstarch and 1 tsp. (5 mL) water. Add chicken and mix well.
2. Finely chop onion and ginger root.
3. In another bowl, combine 1 tsp. (5 mL) cornstarch, sugar, salt, garlic chili sauce, soy sauce and 1 tbsp. (15 mL) water to make the sauce.
4. Heat vegetable oil over medium heat in a 12" (30 cm) frying pan or wok, add chicken slices, onion and ginger root and stir-fry for 2 minutes. When chicken turns white, add sauce; mix well. When the sauce boils, add peanuts and stir-fry for 1 minute.

Serves 4.

Pictured on page 36

* Use a commercial sauce or try the Garlic, Chili and Onion Sauce on page 29.
**Blanched peanuts are available in supermarkets. They are cooked by covering raw peanuts with boiling water and letting them stand for about 5 minutes. Drain and slip the skins off. To dry the nuts, put them on a cookie sheet and bake at 300°F (150°C) for 15-20 minutes, until dry and hot to the touch.

Black Bean Mushroom Chicken

Black bean sauce is a very popular Chinese cooking ingredient. It is in the oriental section of most grocery stores.

½ lb.	chicken breasts	250 g
1 tsp.	cornstarch	5 mL
1 tsp.	water	5 mL
¼ lb.	mushrooms	125 g
1 tsp.	chopped ginger root	5 mL
2	green onions	2
1 tsp.	cornstarch	5 mL
1 tsp.	sugar	5 mL
1 tsp.	soy sauce	5 mL
1 tbsp.	black bean sauce	15 mL
1 tbsp.	water	15 mL
2 tbsp.	vegetable oil	30 mL

1. Cut the chicken breasts into thin slices. In a bowl, mix 1 tsp. (5 mL) cornstarch and 1 tsp. (5 mL) water. Add chicken; mix well.
2. Slice mushrooms. Finely chop ginger root. Cut green onion into 2" (5 cm) lengths.
3. In another bowl, combine 1 tsp. (5 mL) cornstarch, sugar, soy sauce, black bean sauce and 1 tbsp. (15 mL) water to make the sauce.
4. Heat vegetable oil in a frying pan or wok over high heat. Add ginger, stir for ½ minute. Add chicken slices, stir-fry for 2 minutes. When chicken turns white, add mushrooms and sauce. Stir and cook for 2 minutes, until sauce becomes clear. Stir in green onion.

Serves 4. Pictured on page 53

Black Beans

The first recorded soy product in Chinese culinary records was the fermented, salted soft black soybean. Used in soups and sauces, it adds a pungent, salty flavor. Black bean sauce has the added flavors of garlic, scallions and ginger.

Lemon Chicken Breast

A delicious tangy main dish for a Chinese meal or a luxury entrée for two.

1 lb.	chicken breasts	500 g
½ tsp.	salt	2 mL
¼ tsp.	ginger powder	1 mL
3 tbsp.	cornstarch	45 mL
1	egg, beaten	1
1 tbsp.	custard powder (Bird's)	15 mL
2 tbsp.	water	30 mL
1 cup	water	250 mL
1 tbsp.	lemon juice	15 mL
1 tbsp.	sugar	15 mL
3 cups	vegetable oil	750 mL

1. Cut chicken breasts into pieces 2 x 1½" (5 x 4 cm). In a bowl, combine salt, ginger powder, cornstarch and egg. Stir in chicken.
2. Mix custard powder with 2 tbsp. (30 mL) water.
3. In a saucepan, bring 1 cup (250 mL) of water to a boil over high heat; add lemon juice and sugar. Turn heat to medium. Add custard sauce and mix well. When sauce returns to a boil and becomes clear and yellow, turn off the heat.
4. In a large saucepan, heat vegetable oil over high heat* and deep-fry chicken pieces to golden brown. Drain.
5. Pour lemon sauce over chicken pieces.

Serves 4 or 2.

Pictured on page 71

* See note on deep-fat frying on page 56.

Peanut Butter Sesame Chicken

Serve this as part of a cold meal or make a lunch with it

1 tbsp.	minced green onion	15 mL
1	garlic clove	1
1 tbsp.	warm water	15 mL
1 tbsp.	peanut butter	15 mL
1 tsp.	hot chili powder* or Garlic, Chili and Onion Sauce on page 29	5 mL
1 tbsp.	sesame seed	15 mL
1 tsp.	water	5 mL
1 tbsp.	sesame oil	15 mL
1 tbsp.	soy sauce	15 mL
1 tbsp.	sugar	15 mL
2 tsp.	vinegar	10 mL
1/4 tsp.	salt	1 mL
dash	pepper	dash
1 lb.	cooked chicken breasts (see Chicken Broth, page 12)	500 g

1. Mince green onion and garlic. Add 1 tbsp. (15 mL) warm water to peanut butter in a bowl and mix well.
2. In a bowl, mix hot chili powder, sesame seed and 1 tsp. (5 mL) water.
3. Heat sesame oil in a frying pan or wok over medium heat, add hot chili powder mixture. Then turn off heat. Add green onion, garlic, soy sauce, sugar, vinegar, salt, pepper and peanut butter and mix well to make a spicy sauce.
4. Cut cooked chicken breast into fingers about 2" (5 cm) long. Put on a serving plate and pour the sauce over the chicken.

Serves 4.

Pictured on page 72

* See note on hot chili powder on page 27.

Green Pepper with Stir-Fried Chicken

You can multiply quantities if you wish to make more of this mouth-watering dish.

1 lb.	chicken breasts	500 g
1 tsp.	cornstarch	5 mL
1	green pepper	1
1 tsp.	minced ginger root	5 mL
1 tsp.	cornstarch	5 mL
½ tsp.	salt	2 mL
½ tsp.	sugar	2 mL
2 tsp.	soy sauce	10 mL
1 tbsp.	water	15 mL
2 tbsp.	vegetable oil	30 mL

1. Cut chicken breasts into thin slices. In a bowl, mix chicken with 1 tsp. (5 mL) cornstarch.
2. Cut the green pepper into strips. Mince ginger root.
3. In a bowl, combine 1 tsp. (5 mL) cornstarch, salt, sugar, soy sauce and water to make the sauce.
4. Heat vegetable oil in a frying pan or wok over medium heat. Add minced ginger and chicken slices; stir-fry for 2 minutes. When chicken slices turn white, add green pepper and sauce and stir-fry about 2 minutes.

Serves 4.

Pictured on page 53

Green Onion Ginger Chicken

Enjoy this dish with good friends. Your guests will love it.

1 lb.	chicken breasts	500 g
½ tsp.	salt	2 mL
½ tsp.	ginger powder	2 mL
1 tsp.	cornstarch	5 mL
3	green onions	3
¼ tsp.	pepper	1 mL
½ tsp.	soy sauce	2 mL
1 tsp.	cornstarch	5 mL
2 tbsp.	water	30 mL
2 tbsp.	vegetable oil	30 mL
1 tsp.	sesame oil	5 mL

1. Cut chicken breasts into thin slices. In a bowl, combine salt, ginger powder and 1 tsp. (5 mL) cornstarch. Add chicken and mix well.
2. Cut green onion into 2" (5 cm) lengths.
3. In another bowl, combine pepper, soy sauce, 1 tsp. (5 mL) cornstarch and water to make the sauce.
4. Heat vegetable oil in a frying pan or wok over medium heat; add chicken and stir-fry for 2 minutes. When chicken turns white, add sauce and green onion and stir-fry 1 minute. Add sesame oil.

Serves 4. Pictured on page 35

Tomato Ginger Chicken

This dish is a good choice for a party.

1 lb.	chicken breasts	500 g
¼ tsp.	salt	1 mL
½ tsp.	ginger powder	2 mL
1 tsp.	cornstarch	5 mL
2 tbsp.	tomato sauce	30 mL
2 tbsp.	water	30 mL
1 tsp.	cornstarch	5 mL
1 tbsp.	sugar	15 mL
1 tsp.	soy sauce	5 mL
3 tbsp.	vegetable oil	45 mL
½ cup	peas	125 mL

1. Cut chicken breasts into thin slices. In a bowl, mix salt, ginger powder and 1 tsp. (5 mL) cornstarch. Add chicken and mix well.
2. In a bowl, combine tomato sauce, water, 1 tsp. (5 mL) cornstarch, sugar and soy sauce to make the sauce.
3. Heat vegetable oil in a frying pan or wok over medium heat; add chicken slices and stir-fry for 2 minutes. When chicken turns white, add sauce and peas; stir-fry for 2 minutes.

Serves 4.

Pictured on page 54

Chinese Fried Chicken

Crispy and golden, these little chicken morsels can be dipped in a sauce* or served with wine or beer as an appetizer.

1 lb.	chicken breasts	500 g
1	egg	1
½ tsp.	onion powder	2 mL
2 tbsp.	cornstarch	30 mL
½ tsp.	salt	2 mL
½ tsp.	ginger powder	2 mL
½ tsp.	baking powder	2 mL
3 cups	vegetable oil	750 mL

1. Cut chicken into pieces 2 x 1½" (5 x 4 cm).
2. In a bowl, combine egg, onion powder, cornstarch, salt, ginger powder and baking powder. Add chicken and turn to coat well.
3. Heat vegetable oil in a large saucepan over high heat** to 365°F (185°C). Deep-fry chicken, a few pieces at a time. When chicken turns golden brown remove from oil and drain.

Serves 4.

Pictured on page 72

* For dipping sauces, try the Lemon Chicken Breast Sauce on page 68 or the Peanut Butter Sesame Chicken Breast Sauce on page 69, or any of your favorite fruit or spicy sauces.

**See note on deep-fat frying on page 56.

Garlic Beef with Oyster Sauce

This dish is very good with rice or with any of the noodles on pages 46 and 47.

½ lb.	uncooked lean beef	250 g
1 tsp.	soy sauce	5 mL
dash	pepper	dash
2 tbsp.	vegetable oil	30 mL
2 tbsp.	minced onion	30 mL
1	garlic clove	1
1 tsp.	minced ginger root	5 mL
2 tbsp.	oyster sauce	30 mL
1 tsp.	cornstarch	5 mL
1 tbsp.	water	15 mL

1. Cut beef into thin slices, 1 x 1½" (2.5 x 4 cm). In a bowl, combine soy sauce, pepper and 1 tbsp. (15 mL) of the oil. Add beef and marinate for 5 minutes.
2. Mince onion, garlic and ginger root.
3. In another bowl, combine oyster sauce, cornstarch and water to make the sauce.
4. Heat 1 tbsp. (15 mL) vegetable oil in a frying pan or wok over high heat; add beef; stir well. When beef turns brown, add onion, and ginger; stir for ½ minute. Stir in sauce and cook 1 minute.

Serves 4. Pictured on page 35

Fried Lettuce with Beef

You can use any leftovers for a fried rice dish.

½ lb.	uncooked lean beef	250 g
1 tsp.	soy sauce	5 mL
1 tsp.	cornstarch	5 mL
1 tsp.	vegetable oil	5 mL
2	garlic clove	2
½	head lettuce* Romaine, iceberg, etc.	½
1 tbsp.	vegetable oil	15 mL
1 tbsp.	oyster sauce	15 mL
¼ tsp.	salt	1 mL

1. Cut beef into thin slices, 1½ x 1" (4 x 2.5 cm). In a bowl, combine soy sauce, cornstarch and 1 tbsp. (15 mL) vegetable oil. Add beef and marinate for 5 minutes.
2. Mince garlic. Shred lettuce.
3. Heat 1 tbsp. (15 mL) vegetable oil in frying pan or wok over high heat. Add beef; stir-fry for 2 minutes. When beef turns brown, add garlic and oyster sauce; stir-fry for 1 minute. Add lettuce and salt; stir-fry for 2 minutes.

Serves 4.

Pictured on page 53

* See note on lettuce on page 14.

Green Onion Garlic Beef

Quick and easy to prepare – this dish is tasty and has a wonderful aroma.

½ lb.	uncooked lean beef	250 g
1 tsp.	soy sauce	5 mL
1 tsp.	sugar	5 mL
1 tsp.	cornstarch	5 mL
2 tbsp.	vegetable oil	30 mL
4	green onions	4
1	garlic clove	1
¼ tsp.	salt	1 mL

1. Cut beef into thin slices, 1½ x 1" (4 x 2.5 cm). In a bowl, combine soy sauce, sugar, cornstarch and 1 tbsp. (15 mL) vegetable oil. Add beef and marinate for 5 minutes.
2. Cut green onion into 2" (5 cm) lengths. Mince garlic.
3. Heat 1 tbsp. (15 mL) vegetable oil in frying pan or wok over high heat. Add beef; stir-fry for 2 minutes. When beef turns brown, add green onion and salt; stir-fry for 1 minute.

Serves 4.

Pictured on page 18

Variation: To make Green Onion Garlic Beef Noodles, mix this recipe into any of the noodles on pages 46 and 47.

Green Pepper with Soy Sauce Beef

This stir-fried green pepper with beef is very simple and very tasty.

½ lb.	uncooked lean beef	250 g
1 tsp.	soy sauce	5 mL
1 tsp.	sugar	5 mL
1 tsp.	cornstarch	5 mL
1 tsp.	vegetable oil	5 mL
1	green pepper	1
1	garlic clove	1
2 tbsp.	vegetable oil	30 mL
¼ tsp.	salt	1 mL

1. Cut beef into thin slices, 1½ x 1" (4 x 2.5 cm). In a bowl, combine soy sauce, sugar, cornstarch and 1 tsp. (5 mL) vegetable oil. Add beef and marinate 5 minutes.
2. Cut green pepper into bite-sized pieces. Finely chop garlic.
3. Heat 2 tbsp. (30 mL) vegetable oil in a frying pan or wok over high heat. Add garlic and beef; stir-fry for 2 minutes. When beef turns brown, add green pepper and salt. Stir-fry for 2 minutes.

Serves 4.

Pictured on page 71

Variation: To make Rainbow Peppers with Soy Sauce Beef, use ⅓ of each of yellow, red and green peppers to add beautiful color.

Celery Chili Beef

This typical Chinese way of cooking celery keeps it crisp and colorful.

½ lb.	uncooked lean beef	250 g
1 tbsp.	chopped onion	15 mL
1 tsp.	minced ginger root	5 mL
½ lb.	celery	250 g
1 tbsp.	soy sauce	15 mL
1 tsp.	sugar	5 mL
½ tsp.	vinegar	2 mL
1 tsp.	water	5 mL
2 tbsp.	vegetable oil	30 mL
1 tsp.	hot chili powder* or Garlic, Chili and Onion Sauce on page 29	5 mL

1. Cut beef into 2" (5 cm) long strips.
2. Mince onion and ginger.
3. Cut celery into diagonal slices.
4. In a bowl, combine soy sauce, sugar, vinegar and water to make the sauce.
5. Heat vegetable oil in a frying pan or wok over high heat. Add beef; stir-fry for 3 minutes, until the water in the beef evaporates. When beef turns brown, add onion, ginger and chili powder; stir-fry for 1 minute. Add celery and stir-fry for 2 minutes. Add sauce and stir for 2 minutes.

Serves 4.

Pictured on page 53

* See note on hot chili powder on page 27.

Beef-Fried Cucumber

The fresh aroma and crisp texture of the cucumber add zest to this beef dish.

½ lb.	uncooked lean beef	250 g
1 tsp.	soy sauce	5 mL
1 tsp.	sugar	5 mL
1 tbsp.	cornstarch	15 mL
1 tsp.	vegetable oil	5 mL
½ lb.	cucumber	250 g
1 tsp.	minced ginger root	5 mL
1 tbsp.	vegetable oil	15 mL
½ tsp.	salt	2 mL
	pepper (optional)	

1. Cut beef into thin slices, 2 x 1" (5 x 2.5 cm). In a bowl, combine soy sauce, sugar, cornstarch and 1 tsp. (5 mL) oil. Add beef and marinate for 5 minutes.
2. Cut cucumber into thin slices. Mince ginger root.
3. Heat 1 tbsp. (15 mL) vegetable oil in a frying pan or wok over high heat. Add ginger and beef; stir-fry for 2 minutes. When beef turns brown, add cucumber and salt; stir-fry for 2 minutes, just until the cucumber is tender-crisp. DO NOT overcook. Add pepper just before serving.

Serves 4.

Pictured on page 54

Variation: Add 2 minced garlic cloves if you enjoy garlic beef. Add the garlic with the cucumber and salt.

Garlic Beef with Broccoli

It is important to add the garlic last to keep the fresh garlic flavor and aroma.

½ lb.	uncooked lean beef	250 g
1 tsp.	soy sauce	5 mL
1 tsp.	sugar	5 mL
1 tsp.	cornstarch	5 mL
1 tsp.	vegetable oil	5 mL
½ lb.	broccoli	250 g
1	garlic clove	1
1	medium carrot	1
1 tsp.	cornstarch	5 mL
2 tbsp.	water	15 mL
½ tsp.	vinegar (optional)	2 mL
3 cups	water	750 mL
2 tbsp.	vegetable oil	30 mL
1 tsp.	salt	5 mL

1. Cut beef into thin slices, 2 x 1" (5 x 2.5 cm). In a bowl, combine soy sauce, sugar, 1 tsp. (5 mL) cornstarch, and 1 tsp. (5 mL) oil. Add beef and marinate for 5 minutes.
2. Cut broccoli into bite-sized pieces. Finely chop garlic. Cut carrot into thin diagonal slices.
3. In another bowl, combine 1 tsp. (5 mL) cornstarch, water and vinegar (if using) to make the sauce.
4. In a saucepan, bring water to a boil over high heat. Add broccoli and carrots; cook for 2 minutes and drain.
5. Heat 2 tbsp. (30 mL) vegetable oil in a frying pan over high heat. Add beef and stir-fry for 2 minutes. When beef turns brown, add broccoli, carrot and salt; stir-fry for 2 minutes. Add sauce and stir well. Cook for 2 minutes. Take the pan off the heat and then add garlic; mix well.

Serves 4.

Pictured on page 18

Tomato Onion Beef

Serve this with Oriental Noodle Soup or rice.

½ lb.	uncooked lean beef	250 g
1 tsp.	soy sauce	5 mL
1 tsp.	cornstarch	5 mL
1 tsp.	vegetable oil	5 mL
1 tbsp.	minced onion	15 mL
2 tbsp.	tomato soup	30 mL
1 tbsp.	sugar	15 mL
1 tsp.	cornstarch	5 mL
2 tsp.	water	10 mL
2 tbsp.	vegetable oil	30 mL
1 tbsp.	peas	15 mL

1. Cut beef into thin slices, 2 x 1" (5 x 2.5 cm). In a bowl, combine soy sauce, 1 tsp. (5 mL) cornstarch, and 1 tbsp. (15 mL) oil. Add beef and marinate for 5 minutes.
2. Mince onion.
3. In another bowl, combine tomato sauce, sugar, 1 tsp. (5 mL) cornstarch and water to make the sauce.
4. Heat 2 tbsp. (30 mL) oil in a frying pan or wok over high heat; add beef and stir-fry for 2 minutes. When beef turns brown, add peas and onion; stir-fry for 1 minute. Add sauce; mix well. Cook 2 minutes.

Serves 4.

Pictured on page 72

Soy Sauce Beef With Onion

Soy sauce plays an important part in Chinese cooking. It is an
especially good marinade for meat.

½ lb.	uncooked lean beef	250 g
1 tsp.	soy sauce	5 mL
1 tsp.	sugar	5 mL
¼ tsp.	pepper	1 mL
1 tbsp.	cornstarch	15 mL
1 tsp.	vegetable oil	5 mL
1	medium onion	1
1 tbsp.	vegetable oil	15 mL
¼ tsp.	salt	1 mL

1. Cut beef into thin slices, 1½ x 1" (4 x 2.5 cm). In a bowl, combine soy sauce, sugar, pepper, cornstarch and 1 tsp. (5 mL) vegetable oil. Add beef and marinate for 5 minutes.
2. Chop onion into small pieces.
3. Heat 1 tbsp. (15 mL) vegetable oil in a frying pan or wok over high heat. Add beef; stir-fry for 2 minutes. When beef turns brown, add onion and salt; stir-fry for 2 minutes.

Serves 4.

Pictured on page 54

Black Beans with Chili Pork

Black beans have a salty pungent flavor which is delicious with pork, chicken, beef and seafood.

½ lb.	uncooked lean pork	250 g
1 tbsp.	soy sauce	15 mL
1 tbsp.	cornstarch	15 mL
1	green onion	1
1 tsp.	minced ginger root	5 mL
1	garlic clove	1
2 tbsp.	vegetable oil	30 mL
1 tsp.	sugar	5 mL
1 tsp.	black bean sauce	5 mL
½ tsp.	hot chili sauce (Asian)	2 mL

1. Cut pork into 1½" (4 cm) long strips. In a bowl, combine soy sauce and cornstarch. Stir in pork and set aside.
2. Cut green onion into 2" (5 cm) lengths. Mince ginger and garlic.
3. Heat vegetable oil in a frying pan or wok over medium heat;, add pork slices and stir-fry for 3 minutes. When pork turns brown, add green onion, ginger and garlic. Stir-fry for 1 minute. When the aroma is evident, add sugar, black bean sauce and hot chili sauce and mix well. Stir-fry for 1 minute.

Serves 4. Pictured on page 72

Onion Broccoli with Pork

Crisp and colorful, this dish is full of flavor and texture.

½ lb.	uncooked lean pork	250 g
1 tsp.	soy sauce	5 mL
1 tsp.	cornstarch	5 mL
1	carrot	1
½ lb.	broccoli	250 g
2 tbsp.	minced onion	30 mL
1 tsp.	minced ginger root	5 mL
1	garlic clove	1
1 tsp.	cornstarch	5 mL
½ tsp.	salt	2 mL
1 tbsp.	water	15 mL
2 cups	water	500 mL
2 tbsp.	vegetable oil	30 mL

1. Cut pork into thin slices, 1½ x 1" (4 x 2.5 cm). In a bowl, mix soy sauce and 1 tsp. (5 mL) cornstarch. Stir in pork; set aside.
2. Cut the carrot into thin diagonal slices. Cut the broccoli into bite-sized pieces.
3. Mince onion, ginger root and garlic.
4. In another bowl, combine 1 tsp. (5 mL) cornstarch, garlic, salt and water to make the sauce.
5. In a saucepan, bring water to a boil over high heat. Add carrots and broccoli; cook for 2 minutes and drain.
6. Heat vegetable oil in a frying pan or wok over high heat. Add pork slices and stir-fry for 2 minutes. When pork turns brown, add onion and ginger; stir-fry for 1 minute. Add carrots and broccoli; stir-fry for 2 minutes. Add sauce; stir-fry for 2 minutes.

Serves 4.

Pictured on page 72

Bok Choy with Pork

Chinese families enjoy this fresh-tasting dish anytime.

½ lb.	uncooked lean pork	250 g
1 tsp.	soy sauce	5 mL
1 tsp.	cornstarch	5 mL
½ lb.	bok choy*	250 g
1 tbsp.	minced onion	15 mL
1 tsp.	minced ginger root	5 mL
2 cups	water	500 mL
1 tbsp.	vegetable oil	15 mL
½ tsp.	salt	2 mL
½ tsp.	sesame oil (optional)	2 mL

1. Cut pork into thin slices, 1½ x 1" (4 x 2.5 cm). In a bowl, combine soy sauce and cornstarch. Stir in pork and set aside.
2. Cut bok choy into 2" (5 cm) long strips.
3. Mince onion and ginger root.
4. In a saucepan, bring water to a boil over high heat. Add bok choy to boiling water and cook for 2 minutes. Drain.
5. Heat vegetable oil in a frying pan or wok over high heat; add onion and ginger and stir-fry for ½ minute. Add pork; stir-fry for 2 minutes. When pork turns brown, add bok choy and salt; stir-fry for 2 minutes. Add sesame oil, if using, just before serving.

Serves 4.

Pictured on page 72

* See note on Chinese cabbage on page 38.

Pork with Egg and Peas

This dish has a beautiful color and wonderful aroma.

½ lb.	uncooked lean pork	250 g
2 tsp.	soy sauce	10 mL
1 tsp.	cornstarch	5 mL
3	eggs	3
2 tbsp.	minced onion	30 mL
2 tbsp.	vegetable oil	30 mL
¼ tsp.	salt	1 mL
2 tbsp.	peas	30 mL

1. Cut pork into thin slices, 1½ x 1" (4 x 2.5 cm). In a bowl, combine soy sauce and cornstarch. Stir in pork and set aside.
2. Beat eggs well in another bowl.
3. Mince onion.
4. Heat 1 tbsp. (15 mL) vegetable oil in a frying pan or wok over high heat, pour in beaten eggs and scramble. When eggs are set, remove from frying pan and set aside.
5. Heat remaining oil in the frying pan or wok over high heat. Add pork slices and stir-fry for 2 minutes. When pork turns brown, add onion, salt, egg and peas. Stir-fry 3 minutes.

Serves 4.

Pictured on page 54

Green Onion Pork

Sugar enhances this combination of savory flavors.

½ lb.	uncooked lean pork	250 g
1 tbsp.	soy sauce	15 mL
1 tsp.	sugar	5 mL
1 tsp.	cornstarch	5 mL
2	green onions	2
2 tbsp.	vegetable oil	30 mL
¼ tsp.	salt	1 mL

1. Cut pork into thin slices, 1½ x 1" (4 x 2.5 cm). In a bowl, combine soy sauce, sugar and cornstarch. Stir in pork; set aside.
2. Cut green onion into 2" (5 cm) lengths.
3. Heat vegetable oil in a frying pan or wok over high heat. Add pork slices and stir-fry for 2 minutes. When pork turns brown add green onion and salt. Stir-fry for 1 minute.

Serves 4.

Pictured on page 54

Variations: To make Green Onion Pork Noodles, mix this dish with any of the noodles on pages 46 or 47. It is equally delicious combined with rice.

Hot Chili Pork Strings

A warm, rich and colorful dish.

½ lb.	uncooked lean pork	250 g
1 tsp.	soy sauce	5 mL
1	carrot	1
1 tsp.	minced ginger root	5 mL
1	garlic clove	1
2 tbsp.	minced onion	30 mL
½ tsp.	vinegar	2 mL
1 tsp.	sugar	5 mL
¼ tsp.	salt	1 mL
½ tsp.	hot chili sauce (Asian) or Garlic, Chili and Onion Sauce on page 29	2 mL
1 tbsp.	water	15 mL
1 tsp.	cornstarch	5 mL
1 tbsp.	vegetable oil	15 mL

1. Cut pork into 1" (2.5 cm) long strings (very thin strips). Mix with soy sauce in a bowl.
2. Cut carrot into matchstick shapes. Mince ginger, garlic and onion.
3. In another bowl, combine vinegar, sugar, salt, hot chili sauce, water and cornstarch to make the sauce.
4. Heat vegetable oil in a frying pan or wok over high heat. Add ginger and garlic and stir-fry for ½ minute. When the aroma is evident, add pork strings and stir-fry for 2 minutes, cooking and separating strings. When pork turns brown, add onion, carrot, and sauce; stir-fry for 2 minutes.

Serves 4.

Pictured on page 35

Zucchini Onion with Pork

Add this flavorful dish to a party menu.

½ lb.	uncooked lean pork	250 g
1 tsp.	soy sauce	5 mL
1 tsp.	cornstarch	5 mL
½ lb.	zucchini	250 g
2 tbsp.	minced onion	30 mL
2 tsp.	minced ginger root	10 mL
1 tbsp.	vegetable oil	15 mL
¼ tsp.	salt	1 mL

1. Cut pork into thin slices, 1 x ½" (2.5 x 1.25 cm). In a bowl, combine soy sauce and cornstarch. Stir in pork and set aside.
2. Cut zucchini into half lengthwise, then slice. Mince onion and ginger root.
3. Heat vegetable oil in a frying pan or wok over high heat. Add ginger and pork slices; stir-fry for 2 minutes, until pork turns brown. Add onion, salt and zucchini and stir-fry about 4 minutes.

Serves 4.

Pictured on page 71

Variation: If you like peas, add 2 tbsp. (30 mL) peas when you add the zucchini.

Onion Green Beans with Pork

Children love this dish with rice.

½ lb.	boneless pork chops	250 g
1 tsp.	soy sauce	5 mL
½ lb.	green beans (see note below)	250 g
2 tbsp.	minced onion	30 mL
2	garlic cloves	2
1 tsp.	minced ginger	5 mL
1 tbsp.	vegetable oil	15 mL
½ tsp.	salt	2 mL
½ cup	water	125 mL

1. Cut pork chops into thin slices, 1½ x 1" (4 x 2.5 cm). Mix with soy sauce.
2. Cut green beans into 2" (5 cm) lengths. Mince onion, garlic and ginger root.
3. Heat vegetable oil in a frying pan or wok over high heat. Stir-fry onion and ginger for ½ minute. Add pork slices; stir-fry for 2 minutes. When pork turns brown, add green beans and salt; stir-fry for 3 minutes. Add water; cover and cook 4–6 minutes. Do not add water if using Chinese long beans; stir-fry only. When water evaporates, add garlic and stir-fry.

Serves 4. Pictured on page 36

Variation: Add potatoes cut in ½" (2 cm) cubes. Add potatoes with the green beans, cook 6–10 minutes. Do not use potatoes with long beans as the cooking time is shorter.

Chinese Long Beans (Yard-Long Beans)

Also called asparagus bean, this legume is really a member of the black-eyed pea family. The flavor is similar to green beans. The smaller beans are younger, more flexible and more tender. Use beans about 18" (46 cm) or less, although they do grow up to 3' (90 cm). Cut into 2" (5 cm) lengths, they are usually stir-fried or sautéed. DO NOT OVERCOOK as they will become mushy. Substitute green beans if necessary.

Green Pepper with Ginger Pork

Green pepper and pork are a delicious combination.

½ lb.	boneless pork chops	250 g
1 tsp.	cornstarch	5 mL
1 tbsp.	soy sauce	15 mL
1	green pepper	1
¼	onion	¼
1 tsp.	minced ginger root	5 mL
2 tbsp.	vegetable oil	30 mL
¼ tsp.	salt	1 mL

1. Cut pork into thin slices, 1½ x 1" (4 x 2.5 cm). In a bowl, combine cornstarch and soy sauce. Stir in pork and set aside.
2. Cut green pepper and onion into bite-sized pieces.
3. Mince ginger root.
4. Heat vegetable oil in a frying pan or wok over high heat. Add pork and ginger and stir-fry for 2 minutes. When pork turns brown, add onion, green pepper and salt; stir-fry for 2 minutes.

Serves 4.

Pictured on page 35

Tomato Pork Cutlets

This is a good recipe to add to a party menu.

½ lb.	uncooked lean pork	250 g
¼ tsp.	salt	1 mL
1	egg, beaten	1
3 tbsp.	cornstarch	45 mL
1 tbsp.	minced onion	15 mL
1	medium tomato	1
2 tbsp.	tomato sauce	30 mL
1 tbsp.	sugar	15 mL
1 tsp.	soy sauce	5 mL
1 tbsp.	cornstarch	15 mL
2 tbsp.	water	30 mL
2 cups	vegetable oil	500 mL

1. Cut pork into thin pieces, 2 x 1½ x ½" (5 x 4 x 1.3 cm). In a bowl, combine salt, egg and 3 tbsp. (45 mL) cornstarch. Stir in pork and set aside.
2. Mince onion. Cut tomato into wedges.
3. In another bowl, combine tomato sauce, sugar, soy sauce, 1 tbsp. (15 mL) cornstarch and water to make the sauce.
4. Heat vegetable oil in a saucepan over high heat and deep-fry* pork pieces in small batches. When pork turns golden brown, remove from oil and drain.
5. Heat 1 tbsp. (15 mL) oil in a frying pan or wok over high heat. Add onion and tomato; stir-fry 2 minutes and add sauce. When sauce is boiling, add pork and stir-fry for 1 minute.

Serves 4.

Pictured on page 53

* See note on deep-fat frying on page 56.

Ginger Celery Pork

This dish goes wonderfully well with cooked rice.

½ lb.	ground pork or beef	250 g
1 tsp.	soy sauce	5 mL
½ tsp.	sugar	2 mL
2 tbsp.	minced onion	30 mL
1 tsp.	minced ginger root	5 mL
½ lb.	celery	250 g
2 tbsp.	vegetable oil	30 mL
½ tsp.	salt	2 mL

1. In a bowl, mix ground pork with soy sauce and sugar.
2. Mince onion and ginger root.
3. Dice celery.
4. Heat oil in a frying pan or wok over high heat. Add onion and ginger root; stir-fry for 1 minute. Add ground pork; stir-fry for 3 minutes. Add celery and salt, mix well and stir-fry for 2 minutes.

Serves 4.

Pictured on page 17

Variations: To make Ginger Celery Pork or Beef Noodles, mix this recipe with any of the noodles on pages 46 and 47. It is also very good combined with cooked rice.

Ginger Garlic Liver

This dish is very popular in China. Besides being tasty, liver is thought to be helpful for one's eyesight.

½ lb.	pork liver	250 g
½ tsp.	ginger powder	2 mL
¼ tsp.	pepper	I mL
I tbsp.	minced onion	15 mL
2	garlic cloves	2
½	green pepper	½
I tsp.	cornstarch	5 mL
¼ tsp.	salt	I mL
I tbsp.	soy sauce	15 mL
¼ tsp.	vinegar	I mL
I tbsp.	water	15 mL
2 tbsp.	vegetable oil	30 mL

1. Cut liver into thin slices. In a bowl, mix ginger powder and pepper. Stir in liver and set aside.
2. Mince the onion and garlic. Cut the green pepper into bite-sized pieces.
3. In another bowl, combine cornstarch, salt, soy sauce, garlic, vinegar and water to make the sauce.
4. Heat vegetable oil in a frying pan or wok over high heat. Add liver; stir-fry for 3 minutes. When liver turns brown, add onion and green pepper; stir-fry for 2 minutes. Add sauce and mix well. Stir-fry for 2 minutes.

Serves 4.

Pictured on page 72

Deep-Fried Garlic Ribs

This is a wonderful main dish for a Chinese meal. It is also delicious as an appetizer.

1 lb.	spareribs	500 g
1 tsp.	salt	5 mL
1	egg, beaten	1
½ tsp.	ginger powder	2 mL
½ cup	cornstarch	125 mL
3 cups	vegetable oil	750 mL
¼ tsp.	garlic powder	1 mL

1. Cut spareribs into pieces, 2 x 1½" (5 x 4 cm). In a bowl, combine salt, egg, ginger powder and cornstarch. Stir in spareribs.
2. Heat vegetable oil in a saucepan over high heat*, add spareribs, in small batches and deep-fry for 4 minutes, or until they turn golden. Remove ribs from oil and drain.
3. Sprinkle with garlic powder.

Serves 4.

Pictured on page 36

* See note on deep-fat frying on page 56.

Menu Suggestions

 ## Menus for One:

Yang Zhou Fried Rice, page 43
OR Spinach Egg Noodle Soup, page 24
OR Oriental Pork Noodles, page 48
OR Chinese Cold Noodles, page 45

 ## Menus for Two:

1. Tomato Onion Beef, page 83
   Garlic Chicken with Cucumber, page 65
   Tomato Egg Soup, page 26
   Boiled Rice, page 11

2. Pork with Egg and Peas, page 88
   Onion Tofu, page 55
   Peanut Butter Noodles, page 49
   Cream of Corn Egg Soup, page 25

3. Green Onion Ginger Chicken, page 73
   Stir-Fried Vegetables, page 32
   Donggua Ham Soup, page 23
   Boiled Rice, page 11

Menus for Three:

1. Garlic Beef with Oyster Sauce, page 76
   Soy Sauce Eggplant, page 41
   Green Pepper with Ginger Pork, page 93
   Daikon and Vermicelli Soup, page 15
   Boiled Rice, page 11

2. Deep-Fried Garlic Ribs, page 97
   Black Bean Mushroom Chicken, page 67
   Ginger Pork with Tofu, page 59
   Meatball Cucumber Soup, page 22
   Boiled Rice, page 11

 Menus for Four:

1. Ginger Beef with Tofu, page 58
   Cauliflower with Tomato Sauce, page 39
   Onion Broccoli with Pork, page 86
   Oriental Pork Noodles, page 48
   Won Ton Cucumber Soup, page 20

2. Fried Lettuce with Beef, page 77
   Egg Custard with Green Onion, page 50
   Bok Choy with Pork, page 87
   Chinese Fried Chicken, page 75
   Tomato Egg Soup, page 26

 Menus for Five:

1. Green Onion Garlic Beef, page 78
   Zucchini Onion with Pork, page 91
   Lemon Chicken Breast, page 68
   Garlic Fried Potatoes, page 42
   Peanut Butter Noodles, page 49
   Won Ton Cucumber Soup, page 20

2. Peanut Butter Sesame Chicken, page 69
   Celery Chili Beef, page 80
   Tomato Pork Cutlets, page 94
   Tofu with Oyster Sauce, page 56
   Sweet and Sour Fish Fillets, page 61
   Pork with Cucumber Soup, page 19

Menu for Six:

Green Onion Pork, page 89
Tomato Ginger Chicken, page 74
Garlic Beef with Brocccoli, page 82
Sweet and Sour Cabbage, page 37
Garlic Vinegar Cucumber, page 28
Shrimp with Lettuce Soup, page 14
Yang Zhou Fried Rice, page 43

 # Spicy Menu for Six:

Garlic Chili Sauce with Chicken, page 66
Hot Chili Pork Strings, page 90
Hot Chili Tofu, page 57
Cabbage with Onion and Vinegar, page 38
Hot Chili Potatoes, page 42
Chili and Sour Soup, page 27

 # Menu for Eight:

Chili and Sour Soup, page 27
Garlic Beef with Broccoli, page 82
Onion Eggs, page 52
Deep-Fried Garlic Ribs, page 97
Chicken Breast with Oyster Sauce, page 64
Black Beans with Chili Pork, page 85
Garlic Gai Lon, page 33
Tomatoes with Sugar, page 29
Onion Tofu, page 55
Boiled Rice, page 11

 # Vegetarian Menu for Four:

Onion Tofu, page 55
Garlic Gai Lon, page 33
Tomatoes with Sugar, page 29
Stir-Fried Vegetables, page 32
Spinach Noodle Soup, page 24

Boiled rice or noodles would be appropriate with any of these menus.

Index

Share *Chinese* HOME-STYLE COOKING

Order *Chinese* HOME-STYLE COOKING at $10.95 per book plus
$3.00 (total order) for postage and handling.

Chinese HOME-STYLE COOKING _____ x $10.95 = $ ____
Shipping and handling charge _____ = $ 3.00
Subtotal _____ = $ ____
In Canada add 7% GST _____ (Subtotal x .07) = $ ____
Total enclosed_____ = $ ____

U.S. and international orders payable in U.S. funds/Price is subject to change.

NAME:_____
STREET:_____
CITY: _____ PROV./STATE _____
COUNTRY _____ POSTAL CODE/ZIP _____

Please make cheque or money order payable to: **Sharon Wong**
P.O. Box 1026
Regina, Saskatchewan
Canada S4P 3B2

For fund raising or volume purchase prices, contact **Sharon Wong**
Please allow 3-4 weeks for delivery.

Share *Chinese* HOME-STYLE COOKING

Order *Chinese* HOME-STYLE COOKING at $10.95 per book plus
$3.00 (total order) for postage and handling.

Chinese HOME-STYLE COOKING _____ x $10.95 = $ ____
Shipping and handling charge _____ = $ 3.00
Subtotal _____ = $ ____
In Canada add 7% GST _____ (Subtotal x .07) = $ ____
Total enclosed_____ = $ ____

U.S. and international orders payable in U.S. funds/Price is subject to change.

NAME:_____
STREET:_____
CITY: _____ PROV./STATE _____
COUNTRY _____ POSTAL CODE/ZIP _____

Please make cheque or money order payable to: **Sharon Wong**
P.O. Box 1026
Regina, Saskatchewan
Canada S4P 3B2

For fund raising or volume purchase prices, contact **Sharon Wong**
Please allow 3-4 weeks for delivery.

Chinese
HOME-STYLE
COOKING

BY SHARON WONG

Chinese
HOME-STYLE
COOKING

BY SHARON WONG